C000065861

DOUBLE FEATURE: _

EDGAR & ANNABEL
Sam Holcroft

THE SWAN
DC Moore

Also available in a companion volume:

DOUBLE FEATURE: TWO

NIGHTWATCHMAN
Prasanna Puwanarajah

THERE IS A WAR
Tom Basden

DOUBLE FEATURE: ONE

EDGAR & ANNABEL
Sam Holcroft

THE SWAN
DC Moore

NICK HERN BOOKS

London
www.nickhernbooks.co.uk

A Nick Hern Book

Double Feature: One first published in Great Britain in 2011 as a paperback original by Nick Hern Books Limited, 14 Larden Road, London W3 7ST

Edgar & Annabel copyright © 2011 Sam Holcroft
The Swan copyright © 2011 DC Moore
The authors have asserted their moral rights

Cover artwork (from the original National Theatre poster) design by Charlotte Wilkinson
Cover designed by Ned Hoste, 2H

Typeset by Nick Hern Books, London
Printed and bound in Great Britain by CLE Print Ltd, St Ives, Cambs, PE27 3LE

A CIP catalogue record for this book is available from the British Library

ISBN 978 1 84842 219 3

CAUTION All rights whatsoever in these plays are strictly reserved. Requests to reproduce the texts in whole or in part should be addressed to the publisher.

Amateur Performing Rights

Applications for performance of *Edgar & Annabel*, including readings and excerpts, throughout the world by amateurs (except in North America) should be addressed to the Performing Rights Manager, Nick Hern Books, 14 Larden Road, London W3 7ST, *tel* +44 (0)20 8749 4953,
e-mail info@nickhernbooks.demon.co.uk, except as follows:

Australia: Dominie Drama, 8 Cross Street, Brookvale 2100, *fax* (2) 9938 8695, *e-mail* drama@dominie.com.au

New Zealand: Play Bureau, PO Box 420, New Plymouth, *fax* (6) 753 2150, *e-mail* play.bureau.nz@xtra.co.nz

South Africa: DALRO (pty) Ltd, PO Box 31627, 2017 Braamfontein, *tel* (11) 712 8000, *fax* (11) 403 9094, *e-mail* theatricals@dalro.co.za

Rights of performance by amateurs for *The Swan* (except in North America) are controlled by Samuel French Ltd, 52 Fitzroy Street, London W1T 5JR, *tel* +44 (0)20 7255 4302, *e-mail* plays@samuelfrench-london.co.uk; and they, or their authorised agents, issue licences to amateurs on payment of a fee. It is an infringement of the copyright to give any performance or public reading of the play before the fee has been paid and the licence issued.

Professional Performing Rights

Applications for performance by professionals in any medium throughout the world (and by amateur and stock companies in North America) should be addressed to:

Edgar & Annabel: Casarotto Ramsay and Associates Ltd, Waverley House, 7–12 Noel Street, London W1F 8GQ, *fax* +44 (0)20 7287 9128,
e-mail agents@casarotto.co.uk

The Swan: Alan Brodie Representation Ltd, Paddock Suite, The Courtyard, 55a Charterhouse Street, London EC1M 6HA, *tel* +44 (0) 20 7253 6226, *fax* +44 (0)20 7183 7999, *web* www.alanbrodie.com

No performance of any kind may be given unless a licence has been obtained. Applications should be made before rehearsals begin. Publication of these plays does not necessarily indicate their availability for amateur performance.

FSC
www.fsc.org
MIX
From responsible sources
FSC® C019549

Double Feature: One was first performed at the Paintframe, a specially converted space at the National Theatre, London, on 18 July 2011, with the following casts:

EDGAR & ANNABEL

NICK	Trystan Gravelle
MARIANNE	Kirsty Bushell
MILLER	Damian O'Hare
TARA	Karina Fernandez
MARC	Tom Basden
ANTHONY	Richard Goulding
CLAIRE	Phoebe Fox

THE SWAN

GRACE / AMY	Claire-Louise Cordwell
JIM	Trevor Cooper
RUSSELL	Richard Hope
DENISE	Pippa Bennett-Warner
BRADWELL	Nitin Kundra
CHRISTINE	Sharon Duncan-Brewster

Directors	Polly Findlay
	(*The Swan*)
	Lyndsey Turner
	(*Edgar & Annabel*)

Set, Costume
    & Environment Designer   Soutra Gilmour
Lighting Designer   James Farncombe
Movement Director   Jack Murphy
Fight Director   Bret Yount
Sound Designer   Carolyn Downing

This text went to press before the end of rehearsals and so may differ slightly from the plays as performed.

EDGAR & ANNABEL

Sam Holcroft

Sam Holcroft's plays include *Dancing Bears*, part of the
Charged Season for Clean Break at Soho Theatre and Latitude
Festival; *While You Lie* at the Traverse, Edinburgh; *Pink*, part of
the *Women, Power and Politics* Season at the Tricycle; *Vanya*,
adapted from Chekhov, at The Gate; *Cockroach*, co-produced
by the National Theatre of Scotland and Traverse (nominated
for Best New Play 2008, by the Critics' Awards for Theatre in
Scotland and shortlisted for the John Whiting Award, 2009);
Ned and Sharon at the HighTide Festival; and *Vogue*, part of the
Royal Court's Angry Now event, which transferred to Latitude.
Sam received the Tom Erhardt Award in 2009, and was the
Pearson Writer-in-Residence at the Traverse Theatre, 2009–10.

Characters

NICK, *male, late twenties*
MARIANNE, *female, late twenties*
MILLER, *male, older than Nick and Marianne*
TARA, *female, late twenties*
MARC, *male, late twenties*
ANTHONY, *male, late twenties, similar in appearance to Nick*
CLAIRE, *female, late twenties, similar in appearance to*
   Marianne

Setting

The action moves between Edgar and Annabel's kitchen and various meeting places.

Note on Text

Dialogue in [square brackets] is unspoken.

Scene One

EDGAR *and* ANNABEL's *kitchen.*

Someone has gone to great lengths to artfully blend old with new. Clear signs of affluence sit next to bohemia. There is a recycling bin. A kitchen table with chairs stands in the centre of the room.

MARIANNE *stands at the countertop mixing fresh herbs into a decanter of salad dressing. She licks her fingers. She hums contentedly to herself.*

A key is heard in the lock. MARIANNE *smiles and whisks her dressing. The door opens and* NICK *enters wearing a raincoat. He carries a heavy shoulder bag, an umbrella and a plastic shopping bag.*

NICK. Hi, honey, I'm home.

MARIANNE. Hi, darling.

On seeing him she stops short. He meets her gaze. They stare in startled silence. Eventually NICK *tries to break the silence.*

NICK. Something smells good.

Beat.

Is that fish?

Beat.

Is that fish?

Pause.

Is that...?

MARIANNE. Chicken.

NICK. Fish?

MARIANNE. Chicken.

NICK. Fish.

MARIANNE. Fish.

NICK. I thought so. Smells delicious. No, don't kiss me, I'm soaking wet. It's raining cats and dogs out there.

NICK *retrieves two bound documents from his bag and offers one to* MARIANNE. *She stares at it.*

(*With emphasis.*) I'm sorry I'm late. But I had to stand in a doorway for fifteen minutes.

MARIANNE *takes the document. It is a script. Unless stated otherwise, from hereon in they both read from the scripts.*

My umbrella blew inside out.

MARIANNE *doesn't say her line and so* NICK *continues with his.*

You know how that always makes you feel like a right idiot? (*Beat.*) I know, it's so embarrassing. (*Beat.*) Yeah, I did.

MARIANNE. Did... did you get the salad?

NICK (*relieved*). Yeah, I did.

MARIANNE. You remembered?

NICK. Yes, of course.

NICK *hands her the plastic bag. She takes it.*

The checkout is a nightmare during rush hour; the queue stretched all the way down the aisle.

On opening the plastic bag MARIANNE *appears confused. She then scans her script and, understanding, she reads on.*

MARIANNE. I asked for salad.

NICK. Yeah, I know. I bought a bag of salad.

MARIANNE. These are stir-fry vegetables.

NICK (*feigning surprise*). What? No…?

MARIANNE. This is a bag of stir-fry vegetables.

NICK. It can't be, it looks like salad.

MARIANNE. It's a bag of stir-fry vegetables. Here, it says on the front, 'Shredded vegetables for stir-frying'. Did you read the front?

NICK. I… I…

MARIANNE. Did you even look at what you were buying or did you just grab the first bag that you saw?

NICK. I… I was in a hurry.

MARIANNE. Edgar, can you look at what you're buying?

NICK. Yes.

MARIANNE. Can you please look at what you're buying, Edgar?

NICK. Yes.

MARIANNE. Can you?

NICK. Yes, Annabel.

MARIANNE. Thank you.

MARIANNE *opens the oven and removes the roasting dish inside. They both turn the page;* NICK *fails to do this quietly.*

I have a job too.

NICK. Yes, I know.

MARIANNE. I work just as hard.

NICK. You do.

MARIANNE *walks the roasting dish to the table.* NICK *follows, helping her to hold her script and read.*

I'm sorry.

MARIANNE. But I still find time to read the labels on your food.

MARIANNE *places the roasting dish on the table; in it sits a large roasted chicken.*

NICK. Delicious. Is that…?

MARIANNE. Salmon.

NICK. Delicious.

Pause.

So. How was your day?

MARIANNE. I got some more recycling bags.

NICK. Great.

MARIANNE. I hate having to throw all that plastic away. I don't know how people do it.

NICK. Is there any mayonnaise?

MARIANNE. It's such a waste.

NICK. Mayonnaise?

MARIANNE. It only takes two minutes. It makes me so angry.

NICK. In the fridge?

MARIANNE. Yes, but it's not home-made. I'll get it. (*Approaching with an electric carving knife.*) Would you please carve… the salmon?

NICK. Sure. The news today must have had you spitting?

MARIANNE *slows to a stop.*

MARIANNE. What, in the papers?

NICK. No, on the news.

MARIANNE. I didn't see it.

NICK. They're saying the level of plastic in the ocean is killing a million seabirds a year.

MARIANNE. A million?

NICK. Every year.

MARIANNE. That's awful.

NICK. Isn't it? And just this afternoon the police arrested five more people on charges of anti-government conspiracy. (*With emphasis.*) That's right, five of them.

MARIANNE *stares in alarm.*

But don't worry, if it's anti-government charges we won't be seeing them again. Not a single one. I expect they were conspiring to scare us out of our own city. Well, I'm never leaving this neighbourhood, this is my house now and I'm here to defend it. Against troublemakers.

NICK *switches on the carving knife. The sound rings out. NICK motions to urgently make haste. Covered by the sound, he passes her the shoulder bag and a set of documents. He mouths the words 'Hide them. Hide them now. Where do they go?' MARIANNE is paralysed.*

(*Unscripted.*) Annabel. I can't carry this; I'm trying to carve. Help me.

Finally MARIANNE *takes the bag from him. She hides the bag and documents behind various false panels and in unexpected places in the kitchen.* NICK *switches off the electric carving knife. They stand in silence a moment before returning to their scripts.*

MARIANNE. Right then. Shall we sit?

NICK. Napkins?

MARIANNE. Yes. They're clean out of the wash.

She grabs a roll of paper towels and moves to the table. They both sit.

MARIANNE *coughs to cover the sound of tearing strips of kitchen towel.*

NICK. Hungry?

MARIANNE. Starving. And I do so love salmon... sliced.

Scene Two

A meeting place.

MARIANNE *and* MILLER *alone.*

MARIANNE. Where is he?

MILLER. He's gone.

MARIANNE. Where is he?

MILLER. Where are any of them, Marianne?

MARIANNE. Who else?

MILLER. I can't give you their names.

MARIANNE. There were four others.

MILLER. You don't need their names; they're not coming back.

Beat.

MARIANNE. How?

MILLER. They were in a café and they were overheard.

MARIANNE. What were they saying?

MILLER. Nothing specific.

MARIANNE. Carl didn't talk about the house?

MILLER. They were talking about the election, making jokes.
    That's anti-government conspiracy now.

MARIANNE. You sure that's all they said? I've spent the last
    two days expecting the police to kick my door in.

MILLLER. They're not going to kick your door in; nothing was
    said about the house, about any of the houses. They were just
    talking and they were unlucky. We move on.

MARIANNE. But what if they break him, what if they link Carl
    to me?

MILLER. The paper trail leads nowhere and he's trained, Marianne, he'll withstand it.

NICK *enters*.

Were you followed?

NICK. No.

MILLER. You sure?

NICK. I wasn't followed.

Beat.

MILLER. Okay, listen up. I don't have long. These arrests were meant as warning. And they won't be the last. They'll be aiming to pick us off one by one so that come the election there's no one left to dispute it. Word from above is to keep your head down, no more unwanted attention.

NICK. How do we retaliate?

MILLER. We don't.

NICK. They arrest five of our people and we don't retaliate?

MILLER. No. We're stepping back, that's the plan. We're being vigilant, not reactive, okay? You've got to be extra vigilant, even when you think –

NICK. Why wouldn't we send a warning in response? Otherwise they'll just keep going, we'll just keep disappearing, one by one, like you said.

MILLER. Not if you keep your head down.

NICK. If they know we're intent on retaliation they'll think twice before doing it again.

MILLER. Look, Carl was a friend of mine. I don't take it lightly. But the election's more important than the individual. Our priority, and by extension your priority, is to remain politically legitimate at all costs. We give nothing away, nothing. And that way Adam has a chance of taking us across the finish line, okay? If you suspect yourself of being followed, you call it in. If you suspect yourself of getting comfortable, you call yourself on it. Watch each other; they're going to be listening intently, now is the time for continuity.

MARIANNE. So why have you assigned *him*? If attention to detail is a priority.

NICK. Excuse me?

MARIANNE. While I accept Carl had to be replaced, when a complete stranger walks through my door –

MILLER. It's not your door.

MARIANNE. I also ask for a little continuity.

NICK. I had two hours to prepare –

MARIANNE. And he's nothing like Carl.

NICK. And for half an hour of it I was having my haircut.

MARIANNE. He's slow to pick things up: last night he nearly broke the cutlery drawer looking for the bottle opener, the bottle opener doesn't live in the cutlery drawer.

NICK. I've been there two days.

MARIANNE. I came down and he was trying to get the cork out with a fork.

NICK. So what, they can't see me?

MARIANNE. But they can hear you, every last detail. You make far too much noise when you turn the pages. He can't even turn –

NICK. Hang on a second; if I hadn't turned up, Edgar wouldn't have come home to Annabel that night, would he? And anyone listening would have put two and two together and linked his absence to Carl's arrest. You might've been reunited with him sooner than you'd liked.

Beat.

MARIANNE. He improvises.

NICK. No I don't.

MARIANNE. He does. He started speaking before he opened the script. He made me say we were eating fish. You knew what I was cooking, you'd written chicken.

NICK. I was trying to fill the silence.

MARIANNE. Couldn't you smell it was chicken?

NICK. Your chicken smelt like fish.

MARIANNE. He ad-libs, he says 'Yeah' and 'I know'.

NICK. I don't.

MARIANNE. You do.

NICK. When?

MARIANNE. When it's not in the script.

NICK. That's how normal people speak.

MARIANNE. Edgar doesn't speak like that.

NICK. How can a few words matter – ?

MARIANNE. You sound nothing like him.

NICK. What? Not posh enough?

MARIANNE. No, it's not an accent thing: it's a computer, it can't read accents. It's your rhythm –

MILLER. The computers process the rhythm of human speech, not dialect or pitch, so you can't improvise around –

NICK. It's not like someone's going to notice a few –

MILLER. It's not the surveillance teams we need to worry about, they're working across God knows how many houses. It's about fooling the computers. Don't underestimate the technology: any deviations from the norm, lack of fluency, shifts in volume, certain words. It's all flagged. And if it shows up on the system, someone will play it back. We've got no choice, we work on the assumption everything said in that house has the potential to be played back.

NICK. Sure, okay, but the odd word –

MILLER. No.

NICK. I'm not an idiot, I can –

MILLER. It's too easy to slip up, the transition's the hardest part. So until you learn Edgar's speech pattern, we script it. For your own protection.

NICK. Well, how long's the transition?

MILLER. Depends.

NICK. On what?

MILLER. On how quickly you pick it up. Until then, no improvising, okay? Absolutely no improvising. I include just the right amount of low-level interruption, any more and you're going to get flagged.

NICK. How long are we talking – weeks, months?

MILLER. Long as it takes.

MARIANNE. Judging by your performance so far, it might be a while.

MILLER. Just stick to the script, okay, then there's no way they can accuse you of being anything other than a happily married couple of freelancers who met at university.

NICK. Not sure about happy.

MILLER. I'm sorry?

MARIANNE. What's that supposed to mean?

NICK. If it were me listening, I'd be wondering how a woman suddenly develops a barefaced dislike for her husband overnight. Her disappointment is audible. I mean, unless Annabel is supposed to be a bitch.

MARIANNE. Excuse me?

NICK. Yesterday, in the script, she's supposed to compliment that new overcoat. She's supposed to say it made me look like a country gent. She paused after the first syllable in country.

MARIANNE. I did not.

NICK. They're going to be on the look out for faking it. And she's not... with the sex.

MARIANNE. The sex?

NICK. Yes.

MARIANNE. Did no one tell you, we don't actually have to do it?

NICK. She won't even stand next to me; she's across the other side of the room. I'm having to make the noises on my own. She's not putting in the effort.

MARIANNE. I'm not an actor, I do the best I can.

NICK. That's your best? That's your best effort?

MARIANNE. Yes.

NICK. Is that what you sound like when you. When you have sex, that's what you sound like?

MARIANNE. That's what I sound like.

NICK. Like you're ordering from a menu?

MARIANNE. Have you ever been in a long-term relationship? Have you? Cos this kind of predictability is very normal.

NICK. You're certainly painting a picture of your life here.

MARIANNE. They've been together three years, okay? Three years, okay? That's a long time, and the effort I put in is, is realistic, actually.

MILLER. Okay, all right.

MARIANNE. Actually.

MILLER. All right. This isn't working.

MARIANNE. Exactly, thank you.

MILLER. This is what they call 'bad casting'.

MARIANNE. What?

MILLER. You're much more convincing at each other's throats. We need to make this dynamic work for us.

MARIANNE. You need to find me a new partner.

MILLER. No, I just need a reason for the hostility.

MARIANNE. Surely the most important –

MILLER. You know as well as anyone, the people listening are relationship experts. Couples that stop connecting for no reason are a dead giveaway. It's a sure sign there's been a switch.

MARIANNE. So find me someone who can –

MILLER. He's not being replaced. And we can't afford to wait while you come to terms with it.

NICK. Can't she get a throat infection?

MARIANNE. What?

NICK. Then she just wouldn't talk.

MARIANNE. No, Annabel can't get a throat infection.

MILLER. It's relatively simple; I just need to shift the power balance a little. I'll take care of it, and don't worry, I'll write out the sex.

NICK. Why, what are you going to do?

MARIANNE. You can't change it.

MILLER. It's a matter of earning potential, that's all.

NICK. 'Earning potential'?

MILLER. Right now they both have good jobs, draw a decent salary. They're both financially independent, but also rely on the other for the shared income. They need each other, okay? And while that stands, there's no reason for anything other than regular, if uninspiring, sex. We have to upset that natural order.

MARIANNE. So Edgar should lose his job.

NICK. What?

MARIANNE. He'll get depressed. It'll lower his sex drive.

NICK. Why doesn't she lose her job?

MARIANNE. It doesn't work the other way round.

NICK. So you're telling me if you lost your job the first thing you'd want is a shag?

MILLER. If Annabel lost her job *she* might not want sex, but Edgar still would. In fact, he might even want more, what with her being so teary and clinging to him for reassurance. Long term it might do the same damage, yes, but in the short term he'd want to comfort her and most men consider sex a comfort.

MARIANNE. Unfortunately.

NICK. That's bullshit.

MILLER. Financial mobility is integral to their success as a couple. Annabel might even feel obliged to have more sex with him because she's no longer got financial assets to keep her attractive. But we want to be subtle, we want a promotion. Annabel gets a promotion.

NICK. Annabel?

MILLER. At the same time Edgar expresses dissatisfaction with his own job prospects. He's just turned thirty and his wife's more successful than him; it's perfectly conceivable that he'd have some kind of crisis.

NICK. If she's supposed to be so experienced, why can't she have the crisis?

MARIANNE. It doesn't work the other way round.

MILLER (*speaking over them*). It's bad enough I have to rewrite; I'm not wasting time arguing as well. Just get on with it.

NICK. Get on with what, you won't allow us to do anything?

MILLER. Your job.

NICK. I thought my job was to –

MILLER. Your job is to draw as little attention to yourself as possible. Your job is making this transition as seamless as possible. (*To* MARIANNE.) Your job is to trust that, in the absence of Carl, we have chosen the right man to play Edgar. Nick, allow me to introduce Marianne. Marianne, this is Nick; he is ex-army. An explosives expert. Unless either of you want to go the way of Carl, you keep your head down until the election; if it doesn't go our way, then we use your expertise. But you need to last that long. Okay? Are we agreed? Marianne?

MARIANNE. Fine.

NICK. Fine.

MILLER. Good. Fine.

Scene Three

EDGAR *and* ANNABEL*'s kitchen.*

NICK *stands at the countertop chopping vegetables. He chops in stony silence. The key is heard in the lock. He begins chopping more vigorously. The door opens and* MARIANNE *enters. When the door is closed she slides a script out of her bag. She forces a smile. Unless stated otherwise, they both read from their scripts.*

MARIANNE. Hi, honey.

NICK (*without turning*). Hi.

MARIANNE. Something smells delicious. What is it?

NICK (*still without turning*). Stir-fry vegetables.

MARIANNE. Oh, great. Thanks, babe.

NICK *continues to chop.* MARIANNE *retrieves materials for the resistance from her handbag: petrochemicals, weaponry, wiring, etc., and secretes them around the room as she speaks.*

Just vegetables?

NICK. Sorry?

MARIANNE. No chicken?

NICK. No.

MARIANNE. Or prawns?

NICK. Nope.

MARIANNE. Okay…

NICK. Something wrong with vegetables?

MARIANNE. No, nothing.

NICK. Then why the voice?

MARIANNE. What voice?

NICK. You don't want a vegetable stir-fry?

MARIANNE. No, it's just… you should have rung me; I would have picked something up.

NICK. I wanted to cook a vegetable stir-fry.

MARIANNE. You didn't have to use it just because it was in the fridge.

NICK. I didn't.

MARIANNE. Honey…

NICK. I didn't.

They both turn the page; NICK *achieves this silently.*

MARIANNE. If you wanted prawns you could have asked me to buy them; it would've been my pleasure.

NICK. We should be eating more vegetarian meals.

MARIANNE. Yes, but…

NICK. We've talked about how we should be eating more vegetarian meals.

MARIANNE. I know, but –

NICK. So don't insist on having everything with prawns.

Beat.

MARIANNE. There aren't even any mushrooms.

NICK. What?

MARIANNE. You haven't even got any mushrooms. Are we just having cabbage, peppers and noodles?

NICK. And mangetout.

MARIANNE. Four mangetout. (*Picking up the packet.*) There are four mangetout in here. (*Beat.*) Is there any sauce?

NICK. Soy sauce.

MARIANNE. *Soy sauce?*

NICK. And butter.

MARIANNE. Oh good, that's all right then, for a second there I was worried you hadn't thought this through, but now I understand, we have *butter*. (*Beat.*) Why don't I just order us a Chinese?

NICK. No, thank you.

MARIANNE. You'll eat that over a real Chinese?

NICK. Yes, thanks.

MARIANNE *reaches for a bottle of wine and glass on the countertop. In doing so she gets in* NICK*'s way.*

MARIANNE. Oh, come on; just let me buy us dinner. There's no point in being a martyr.

NICK. What? What do you want?

MARIANNE. What?

NICK. I'm trying to cook, what do you need?

MARIANNE. I want a glass of wine.

NICK. Well, I'll get it, ask me and I'll get it.

MARIANNE. What's the matter?

NICK. I can't cook if you're all... up in my...

MARIANNE (*reaching for the bottle*). I'm just getting a glass of wine.

NICK (*pushing her back and reaching for the wine*). Let me do it.

MARIANNE. Stop it.

NICK. Can you just... just give me your glass?

NICK *grabs her glass to pour the wine.*

MARIANNE. Stop it, you're being so –

NICK *accidently spills wine all over her script.*

(*Unscripted.*) Fuck's sake, Nick!

Beat.

Edgar. Fuck's sake, Edgar.

They stare at each other immobilised.

NICK (*attempting a rescue*). Don't lose your temper with me!

NICK *is off script until stated otherwise.* MARIANNE *shakes her sodden script; the pages are glued together. She looks at him, paralysed with panic.*

Don't be so... patronising.

MARIANNE. I... I...

NICK. I have a job too.

MARIANNE *searches for words.*

I work just as hard.

MARIANNE. Yes... I know.

NICK. And I still manage to come home... and, and try and cook you dinner. You can't even be nice about it.

MARIANNE. I... No...

NICK. And then you have a go at me. That's, that's rich.

MARIANNE. I'm sorry.

NICK. I was doing my best.

MARIANNE. I know.

NICK. I was trying.

MARIANNE. I'm sorry.

> NICK *turns back to his script to find a place to pick up the thread*.

NICK (*reading from the script*). Sorry isn't good enough.

> *He approaches and shares his script; pointing to her line. They have to stand close*.

MARIANNE (*finding the line*). Edgar...

NICK. Don't '*Edgar*' me.

MARIANNE. Don't be upset.

NICK. Of course I'm upset! If I came home and criticised your cooking I'd never hear the end of it.

MARIANNE. I know, but you have to admit you're very sensitive at the moment. I feel like I'm walking on eggshells.

NICK. Annabel, you said you wanted to order a takeaway.

MARIANNE. I know, but...

NICK. While I was cooking.

MARIANNE. I didn't think...

NICK. I was cooking for you.

> MARIANNE *falls silent*.

Let me know when my wife comes home. I didn't marry a bitch.

NICK *and* MARIANNE *look at one another. As the script dictates,* NICK *turns and exits.* MARIANNE *stands alone.*

Scene Four

A meeting place.

NICK *and* MARIANNE *await* MILLER. MARIANNE *paces.*

MARIANNE. Shit.

NICK. All they heard was a name.

MARIANNE. Shit.

NICK. It's not even distinctive, 'Nick'.

MARIANNE. I can't believe I...

NICK. It's fine.

MARIANNE. It's not.

NICK. It's fine. Marianne?

MARIANNE. I can't...

NICK. Are you all right?

MARIANNE. I... Yes, I just...

NICK. You sure?

MARIANNE. I think I'm having a sugar low. And I... I can't sit down in here.

NICK. Here. (*Taking a can of Coke out of his pocket and passing it to her.*) Have this.

MARIANNE. No, I...

NICK (*opening the can*). Have it.

MARIANNE. I'm fine.

MARIANNE *paces before squatting on the ground.*

NICK. Don't sit on the ground.

MARIANNE. No, I'm… I'm…

MARIANNE *bows her head and rocks slightly.* NICK *squats on the ground next to her.*

NICK. Marianne? Take it.

MARIANNE. I… I'm… Thank you.

MARIANNE *drinks; they remain a small distance from each other, squatting close to the ground.*

NICK. Okay?

MARIANNE. I'm… (*Drinking.*) Sometimes I… If I don't eat I… Since I was a little girl. I come over all… shaky, I get the shakes.

NICK. Sure.

MARIANNE. That's why I eat cheese biscuits at night; my, my metabolism is so fast if I don't, I, I feel sick in the morning.

NICK. Okay.

MARIANNE. That's why.

NICK. Sure.

MARIANNE. That's why.

MARIANNE *drinks.*

NICK. I drink about a litre of Coke a day.

MARIANNE. I'm sorry?

NICK. I drink about a litre of Coke every day. That's why I… piss as much as I do.

MARIANNE. Oh. Right. (*Beat.*) Why don't you…?

NICK. Why don't I cut back?

MARIANNE. Yeah.

NICK. It's a… it's an army thing, I think. I just used to drink shitloads of Coke. Not even real Coke, just like whatever they got on tap, you know?

MARIANNE. Sure.

NICK. I try and cut down but…

MARIANNE. Uh-huh.

NICK. It's…

MARIANNE. Yeah.

NICK. Yeah.

MARIANNE. My mum used to say it was – with the cheese biscuits – it was psychological.

NICK. Right.

MARIANNE. But I can't, I literally can't get to sleep unless, unless I've…

NICK. Unless you've had some cheese biscuits.

MARIANNE. Right.

NICK. You do what you got to do.

Beat.

MARIANNE. Why did you leave? The army?

NICK. It wasn't for me.

They squat in silence.

MARIANNE. I'm sorry. There's no excusing what I did.

NICK. It's all right.

MARIANNE. No, there's no excuse.

NICK. It's okay.

Pause.

If I were him I'd punch myself in the face.

MILLER *enters*.

MILLER. What are you doing?

Marianne?

MARIANNE. I was just… I had a sugar…

MILLER. What are you doing, Marianne?

MARIANNE. I'm sorry. I screwed up.

MILLER. It's not just Nick you're putting at risk.

MARIANNE. I know that.

MILLER. It's yourself; the house; the whole organisation.

MARIANNE. I know.

MILLER. It's bad enough you raised your voice. It's a miracle if they didn't flag it, cos our boys sure heard it. They picked up the signal, called me straight away. Have you heard anything in the house, any feedback on the phone, sounds, flickering lights, anything?

MARIANNE. No.

MILLER. Nothing?

MARIANNE. No.

MILLER. Then you're lucky. You're lucky the police haven't kicked your door in.

NICK. It wasn't all her fault.

MILLER. She called her husband another man's name.

NICK. I know, but –

MILLER. That's the worst she could have done.

NICK. I spilt wine on her script. It's not her fault I was clumsy; I'm clumsy.

MARIANNE. You're not.

NICK. I am.

MARIANNE. No, I overreacted.

NICK. No you didn't.

MARIANNE. I did.

MILLER. Well, I couldn't give a fuck which of you is the more inept. You cannot bring suspicion on the house. That is unacceptable. You have four gallons of petrochemicals under your roof.

MARIANNE. We weren't trying to –

MILLER. Don't argue, listen to me: if you expose the house you'll cost us the election. Adam may be the best leader we ever had, but that's not enough on its own. The moment they prove an association between the party and one of our houses, we're out the running. We don't get a look-in for another seven years. All this work, the gain in the polls, riding the backlash, it's all for nothing. The only way we can keep gaining ground is to keep Adam clean. And then maybe, just maybe, we might have a chance at winning.

NICK. We're not going to win.

MILLER. We'll get a decent share, at the very least.

NICK. What, thirty per cent of the vote? Thirty-five?

MILLER. That's a twenty per cent gain.

NICK. Still nothing like a majority.

MILLER. Could be more.

NICK. Not even close.

MILLER. The aim is to gain ground.

NICK. How can the aim be to finish no better than we start –

MILLER. We're moving forward.

NICK. – in the minority. We're still in the minority. We still don't have a free press. We're still spending two forty on a pint of milk.

MILLER. We'll have political –

NICK. And instead of putting the shit up them and showing them we won't stand for it, we're sending the message, loud and clear, to them and the rest of the world, 'Don't worry, everybody, we're fine, totally fine; in fact we're loving this shitbox of a situation, we can't get enough brutality. I love a good kidney-punch, me. What a privilege! What a… what a privilege. Completely, completely fine. No problem. No fucking problem here…'

MILLER. Nick, we – [can't afford to get emotional.]

NICK. Let me do the job I'm trained for.

MILLER. This is the job you're trained for.

NICK. I'm sleeping under the same roof as four gallons of petrochemicals, let me use them!

MILLER. Not yet.

NICK. Now, let's send a signal now, and if they come down on us like a ton of bricks we'll be showing them for who they really are. People'll take to the streets. We'll be united. We'll have our uprising.

MILLER. Any idiot can make a banner and join a demonstration.

NICK. I'm not saying I'll –

MILLER. You are not a teenager in an angry T-shirt; you're a trained operative.

NICK. I'm a soldier.

MILLER. But we are not an army.

NICK. Then what are we?

MILLER. We are a political movement. And for the first time in years, the door is open to us to make political gain. We must be seen to take it. Nobody will support us if we are considered terrorists. If the time comes for action it must be justified.

NICK. What more justification – ?

MILLER. While we're still able to campaign – [it's not justified.]

NICK. Call this a campaign?

MILLER. So long as they continue to make a show of this being a free election, we can't take action, course we can't.

NICK. But if –

MILLER. But nothing, okay? We're committed to this course. And might I remind you, I've been working through the night to rewrite a week's worth of scripts because the two of you couldn't bring yourselves to moan in the name of justice. And when I ask you to be discreet, you're spilling your wine and giving each other away. Now I know you can do better than that, that's why you signed up. Cos it's disgusting. It's disgusting that our friends are arrested for telling a joke. It's disgusting that doctors are surrendering our records. It's disgusting that nobody knows who to trust. I don't want that for my country. Adam doesn't want that. I want to believe it's possible to have fairness, and opportunity and for kids to learn from their teachers not spy on them. And I'll do anything, anything, by any means, to make that happen.

MARIANNE. Yeah.

MILLER. Yes?

NICK. Yes.

MILLER. Then stand either side of the room staring at the wall for all I care, just read the fucking words in front of you!

MILLER *exits*.

Scene Five

EDGAR *and* ANNABEL*'s kitchen.*

NICK *and* MARIANNE *sit at the table to eat. At the top of the scene they go through the motions with eyes glued to their scripts, careful of every word.*

MARIANNE. We don't have any plans this weekend, do we? (*Beat.*) Do we? This weekend? (*Beat.*) So you're not even talking to me now?

NICK. No, we don't have any plans.

MARIANNE. I think we should go to the garden centre. Can you pass the rice?

    NICK *passes the rice without taking his eyes off the script.* MARIANNE *transfers rice without taking her eyes off her script; she misses the plate.*

    I want to get another azalea for the front. You know what I mean by an azalea? Edgar?

NICK. Is it the one with flowers?

MARIANNE. It's the red bush by the gate. I want one on the other side, don't you think? A pink one. But a nice pink, not a garish pink or what Emily would call 'feminine hygiene', but something in between. Like carnation or cherry blossom, don't you think?

NICK. Tremendous.

MARIANNE. But of course I don't want to be one of those women whose garden is just full of pink. I couldn't bear to be one of those women. Shall I finish this?

    MARIANNE *scrapes the bowl.*

But the thing is, my camellia keeps dying and Emily says I need to replace it with something hardy like a rose, but that just means more pink.

NICK. Telly?

MARIANNE. What?

NICK. Telly supper? Don't you think?

NICK *leans across and switches on the television. The screen of the television is not visible to the audience. A generic news programme plays at a low level. Covered by the sound,* NICK *and* MARIANNE *turn to the whiteboard.*

MARIANNE *writes:* 'Maternal Grandmother?'

NICK *writes in response:* 'Alice.'

MARIANNE *nods and writes:* 'Annabel's degree?'

NICK: 'Geography.'

MARIANNE: 'Edgar, circumcised?'

NICK *hesitates then nods.* MARIANNE *writes:* 'Grounds?'

NICK: 'Hygiene.'

MARIANNE *nods and writes:* 'Nicknames?'

NICK: 'Eggers.'

MARIANNE *nods and writes:* 'And?'

NICK: 'Edmegeddon.'

MARIANNE *nods:* 'And Annabel?'

'Hitler.'

MARIANNE *stifles a laugh. She writes:* 'It's my birthday.'

NICK *draws her a cake with candles. She smiles. He then mouths the words to the song 'Happy Birthday'.*
MARIANNE *bursts out laughing. She tries to stifle the laugh but she is beset by a fit of giggles.* NICK *grabs the remote and turns up the volume to cover their laughter.*
MARIANNE *tries to stuff her napkin in her mouth.*

NEWSREADER. The Government has issued a statement to
warn that security in the capital will be increased tonight
following the arrest of opposition leader, Adam Glencannon.
Glencannon was arrested at his home earlier today on
charges of conspiracy and tax evasion. According to the
public prosecutors office, Glencannon has been under
investigation since the beginning of the year when a
subsidiary of his publishing house, HorsePerrin, filed for
insolvency. If found guilty, Glencannon will face up to four
years in prison. A source close to the party has revealed that
it is unlikely the opposition will be able to field another
candidate with the election just two months away. (*Beat*.)
The Government today announced plans to bring forward
legislation to abridge the right to assembly.

Scene Six

EDGAR *and* ANNABEL*'s kitchen.*

MARIANNE *and* NICK *prepare for guests. They arrange
crisps and dips in bowls and assemble equipment for karaoke.*

MARIANNE. Did you remember the guacamole?

NICK. Yes.

MARIANNE. Definitely guacamole?

NICK. I checked the label and everything.

MARIANNE (*checking her watch*). Can you leave it on the side
with the hummus? Not the table, on the side. I'm going to
decant them.

NICK. Into what?

MARIANNE. Bowls.

NICK. They're already in bowls.

MARIANNE. China bowls. It's nicer.

NICK. It's more washing-up.

MARIANNE. Can you just leave them, please?

NICK *leaves the guacamole on the side.*

Shit.

NICK. What?

MARIANNE. I didn't put the wine in the fridge; they'll be here any minute.

NICK. I'll put in the freezer.

MARIANNE. There isn't time, just serve it with ice.

MARIANNE *checks her watch again. They look at each other, unsure what to do; they have run out of script.*

There is a knock at the door.

(*Relieved.*) They're here!

NICK. Great. Great.

MARIANNE *answers the door.* TARA *and* MARC *stand on the other side.* MARC *carries a box of wine and* TARA *carries a large handbag.*

TARA. Hello!

MARIANNE. Hi!

They kiss.

Hi, Henry.

MARC. Hello, gorgeous.

They greet each other. TARA *enters and approaches* NICK; *she scrutinises the new recruit. Once the door is closed, both* TARA *and* MARC *take out their matching scripts. Unless stated otherwise they all read from scripts.*

TARA. Darling, hi.

NICK. Emily!

TARA. How's things?

NICK. Good, good, thank you.

MARC. Ah. Cock of the walk.

NICK. All right, mate.

MARC. Got your victory swagger.

NICK. Not a swagger, I think I strained my bloody groin.

MARC. Yeah, I know, I could hardly walk afterwards.

NICK. Good game, though.

MARC. I'll get you next time.

NICK. Fighting talk.

MARC. Save the fighting for the squash, mate.

NICK. Sounds like you mean business.

MARC. We'll have to see.

NICK. A beer, mate?

MARC. Yeah, that'll do nicely.

MARIANNE. Emily, there's wine or vodka?

TARA. White wine?

MARIANNE. Yes, but it's warm. D'you want it with ice?

TARA. Lovely, thank you. Oooh, crisps. Yummy.

MARIANNE (*pouring* TARA *a glass of wine*). I made a pâté, a chicken liver pâté. But Edgar came home from work late last night and ate the lot.

TARA. Edgar!

MARIANNE. Just swoops in like a vulture, and eats it all up!

TARA. You didn't?

MARIANNE. He did.

NICK. I did, yeah.

MARC. Risky move.

TARA. You bad man.

MARC. Worth it, though, right?

NICK. Definitely.

MARC. Bet it was.

NICK. Yeah, I really like pâté.

MARIANNE. Don't we all, but it's just crisps and dips I'm afraid.

MARC (*taking a beer from* NICK). Thanks, man.

TARA. Darling, this guac is delish.

MARC. God, I love the guac. Give me some of that bad boy.

MARIANNE. No, I meant to decant it.

TARA. I'm the same, makes it look home-made, right? But don't bother, babe, it's just us – save on washing-up. We brought some snacks too. (*Pointedly.*) Henry, give them to her.

MARC *carefully unpacks bomb-making materials secreted inside everyday snacks and containers. He handles each item with precise care.*

MARIANNE. I'm sorry there's no pâté.

TARA. Don't be ridic, honey, we're not hungry. We just came from lunch with my mum.

NICK. Fun.

MARC. Yeah, she's a riot.

MARIANNE. How's she doing? She well?

TARA. Yeah, but you know my mum, always something to worry about. It used to be that my sister was going to die a spinster.

MARIANNE. I remember.

TARA. I was like, 'Mum, this isn't *Pride and Prejudice*.'

She laughs; they all laugh to cover the sound of turning a page of their scripts.

I mean, she's an actuary. She earns more money than God. What does she need a husband for? (*To* MARC.) Just kidding, babe, I've no idea how to check the tyre pressure. Anyway, now that she's finally about to walk down the aisle, Mum's turning her attention back on me. She wants me to move to my sister's neighbourhood.

MARIANNE. Oh, really?

MARC (*to* NICK). Nice beer, man.

NICK. Thanks.

MARC. Malty.

TARA. Yeah, she's gone and bought a flat in one of those massive buildings with the pillars outside.

MARIANNE. Wow.

TARA. You couldn't pay me to live there.

MARIANNE. No?

TARA. We wouldn't live there, would we?

MARC. What?

TARA. Definitely not. Seriously, do you need that much guacamole?

MARC. Huh?

TARA. You know, it's just not got enough personality for me. I want to live somewhere interesting, somewhere diverse, somewhere with some other heritage than money, you know?

MARIANNE. Sure.

TARA (*to* NICK). Don't you agree?

NICK. Yeah, I mean sometimes you just want an authentic Jamaican curry.

TARA. Exactly, I don't want to live my whole life eating the food my mother cooked me.

MARC. Nobody wants to eat the food your mother cooked you.

MARIANNE. Can you imagine?

TARA. Bor-ing.

MARC. What's this?

MARIANNE. Hummus, babe.

TARA. I want my kids to know there's more than two ways of doing potatoes. You see yourselves having kids, right?

MARIANNE. Of course.

TARA. How many?

MARIANNE. Three.

MARC. Good going, mate.

NICK. Hang on, three?

MARIANNE. Yes, two boys and a girl. Not because boys are better. Because. Boys aren't better.

TARA. No.

MARIANNE. It's just a good dynamic.

TARA. It's a really good dynamic. Anyway, we're so looking forward to my sister's wedding.

MARIANNE. When is it?

TARA. Well, that's the thing, I've no idea.

MARIANNE. What do you mean, you've no idea?

TARA. The minister's having dental surgery and so it all depends on when he's recovered.

NICK. They won't settle on a date because of the minister?

TARA. That's right. This particular minister is particularly important to her, so yes, it all depends on our access to him. So we'll just have to wait.

MARC. Yeah, we just have to wait.

MARIANNE. How long?

TARA. Long as it takes.

Short pause.

So, who's ready for a sing-off! Come on! Edgar?

NICK. I think I need another beer first.

TARA. Oh, don't be shy.

NICK. I need another beer.

TARA. He's a bit shy without the beer, isn't he?

MARIANNE. And last night he put away the pâté so he's probably a bit fat too.

TARA. Guess we're going first, my darling.

MARC. Guess so.

TARA. What shall we do? Madonna? Elvis?

MARC moves to the television screen and turns it on, uploading the programme.

NICK. I think we've just got the one with rock ballads.

TARA. That all?

MARIANNE. It's new; we only got the one CD.

TARA. But look at it: it's beautiful.

MARC. Must have set you back a bit.

MARIANNE. I felt like treating myself, you know? Why earn money if you can't spend it?

TARA. Quite right.

MARC. How about...

TARA. No. No, no, no, no…

MARC. This one?

TARA. No… no, no, yes! We have to.

MARC. No we don't.

TARA. Yes we do; it's so… us! Come on. Where's my thingy?

MARC. Hello.

TARA. Give me my microphone.

MARC *hands her a microphone; he takes one for himself.*

Play it, come on, play it! You ready?

MARC. Born ready.

TARA (*to* MARIANNE *and* NICK). Prepare to get yo asses kicked!

MARC *presses play. Starship's 'Nothing's Gonna Stop Us Now' (or similar) begins to play.*

The moment there is music to cover them, NICK *and* MARIANNE *begin to assemble the component parts of a bomb.* MARC *and* TARA *sing at the top of their lungs and egg each other on enthusiastically. At one point* MARIANNE *drops an item.* NICK *stiffens in alarm.* TARA *compensates by raising her volume, and* MARC *drums on the table to mimic the sound.*

(*To* MARC, *speaking.*) Yeah, drumming, nice!

MARC (*speaking*). Thank you!

TARA *takes over drumming, and* MARC *sings.*

NICK *moves fluidly, expertly and with confidence. They work closely together, enjoying the proximity.* MARC *and* TARA *finish the song together.*

At the end of the song, MARIANNE *and* NICK *stop working and applaud* MARC *and* TARA *enthusiastically.* NICK *wolf-whistles.*

TARA. Whoa, yeah!

MARIANNE. Amazing!

MARC. That's my wife! That's. My wife!

TARA. Yeah, baby! You were amazing.

MARC. The singing assassins.

NICK. All right. What's the score?

TARA. Three thousand nine hundred and fifteen! Yeah!

MARC. Eat our dust. Eat it.

MARIANNE. La-me.

TARA. Think you can do better?

MARIANNE. I know we can do better.

TARA. Bring it, bitch.

> MARIANNE *takes* TARA*'s place by the karaoke machine.*
> NICK *stares reluctantly at the microphone being offered him.*

MARIANNE. Come on, babe.

TARA. You don't want to let you wife down now, do you?

> NICK *takes the microphone.*

MARC. That's it, Eggers. Do your worst, my boy!

MARIANNE. You ready?

> NICK *nods; swallows.*

> MARIANNE *presses play and Cyndi Lauper's 'Time After Time' (or similar) begins to play.* MARIANNE *ramps up the volume. As soon as the music plays,* TARA *and* MARC *attempt to pick up where the other two left off.* NICK *directs them from where he stands.*

> MARIANNE *sings the first verse, and then signals for* NICK *to begin.* NICK *sings, off beat, uncertain. They continue to sing together until the end of the song.* NICK *eventually finds his rhythm and relaxes a little. When the song comes to an end,* MARC *and* TARA *clap for them enthusiastically.*

MARC. Look at you.

TARA. Eddy!

MARC. Look at you and your big face.

TARA. You two are on fire. This is actually a competition.

MARC. I'll say. What d'you get?

NICK. Four thousand and twenty-five.

MARIANNE. Oh my God, we won!

MARC. Let me see that.

MARIANNE. I can't believe we won.

NICK (*to* MARC). Four thousand and twenty-five. In your face.

MARC. It's broken. You broke it.

TARA. Rematch! I demand a rematch. We were taking it in easy on you. Just doing you a favour. Henry, get back up here, we're going again. Watch closely. This is how it's done.

TARA selects a song and it begins to play...

Time passes. They sing songs. They build a bomb.

MARC. I don't know about you, but I am totally banjaxed. (*Feigning a yawn.*) Come on, missus, it's time we hit the road. You lost your voice?

TARA doesn't respond.

You doughnut. Come on, up you get.

TARA. Do you like my shoes?

MARC. Your shoes?

TARA. Do you like them? Don't hesitate.

MARC. I didn't, I was about to say –

TARA. He doesn't like my shoes.

MARC. It's time to go.

TARA. What d'you know about shoes anyway?

MARC. All right, up you get.

TARA. The other week he bought orthopaedic trainers.

MARC. I have a bad back.

TARA. He looks like a granny.

MARC. Up you get.

TARA. You look like a granny.

MARC. You look like a granny.

TARA. I do not.

MARC. You're the one who can't lift herself off the floor.

TARA. I can lift myself off the…

MARC. Do it then.

MARIANNE. Wait… take some of the wine.

MARC. No, keep it.

> MARC *helps* MARIANNE *to secure the bomb into the wine case.*

MARIANNE. We can't possibly drink all this.

TARA. Are you sure?

MARIANNE. Absolutely. Besides, we'll only drink it next time we come to yours.

TARA. No, we're busy preparing for the wedding, but you know who'd love a go on your new machine? Leo and Helen.

MARC. They'd love it. And Tom and Suze.

TARA. Yeah, Tom and Suze.

MARC. What about Doug and Franny? They'd love a go.

TARA. Doug and Franny for definite. You should expect to have a lot of dinner parties.

MARC. A lot.

TARA. When I say a lot, I mean *a lot.*

MARC. *A lot of dinner parties.*

TARA. You might want to get another CD.

Beat.

MARC. Right, Jack, let's hit the road.

TARA. Thanks, guys, it was the best.

MARIANNE. No problem. Any time.

MARC (*to* MARIANNE). See you soon, little one.

MARIANNE. Yeah…

TARA. I love you.

NICK. Night, Emily.

TARA. I do, I love you.

MARC. Come on, you old fruit.

TARA. You're one of my favourites.

MARC. Let's get you home before you start kissing the wrong husband.

TARA. Next time…

MARIANNE. Yeah, you'll get us next time.

TARA *and* MARIANNE *look at one another. They embrace. It is a long, heartfelt goodbye. The two men watch them.*

You got everything?

TARA. Yeah, think so.

MARIANNE. You didn't come with a coat?

TARA. No, just my cardi.

MARIANNE. Okay then.

NICK *takes a pen and writes on the back of his script. He holds it up to display the message,* 'Good luck.' MARC *nods.*

Eventually, TARA *and* MARIANNE *separate.*

MARC. Off we go then.

TARA. Where's my shoes?

MARC. You're wearing them, come on. See ya.

MARIANNE. Bye.

NICK. Bye.

> MARC *and* TARA *exit*. NICK *closes the door.*
>
> *A long pause.*
>
> Shall we clear now, or…

MARIANNE. Now.

> *They clear in silence. Every so often they look up to meet each other's gaze.*

NICK. Did you have a good time?

MARIANNE. Sure. You?

NICK. Uh-huh. They're good value.

MARIANNE. Yeah.

NICK. Tara's always…

MARIANNE. Pissed.

> *They clear in silence.*

NICK. They finished all the guacamole.

MARIANNE. Because there wasn't anything else.

NICK. I didn't realise the pâté was for tonight. (*Beat*.) I wouldn't have eaten it if I thought it was.

MARIANNE. When do I make pâté unless we're having a party?

NICK. You don't. You never do.

MARIANNE. You want me to apologise for not having time to make pâté unless it's for a party?

NICK. That's not what I said.

MARIANNE. *You* want an apology from *me*?

NICK. Not for the pâté.

MARIANNE. Then for what?

NICK. For calling me fat.

MARIANNE. I didn't.

NICK. You said I was fat.

MARIANNE. I said *probably* fat. It was a joke.

NICK. Not funny.

MARIANNE. Shame about your sense of humour.

NICK. I have a sense of humour.

MARIANNE. You sure?

NICK. What's the difference between a lawnmower and a mezzo-soprano? Both are better at singing than you.

He kisses her, hard. They pull back. MARIANNE *checks her script.*

MARIANNE. Well, that was unnecessary.

NICK. Then I guess we're even.

MARIANNE. This is about my promotion.

She kisses him. They pull back. NICK *checks his script.*

NICK. That was mean.

MARIANNE. You so enjoy playing the victim, don't – ?

NICK. And you so enjoy feeling self-righteous. You're your mother's daughter all right.

MARIANNE. How dare you? That is such a cheap shot. You know how I feel my mother. (*Checking herself.*) About. You know how I feel *about* my mother. Where are you going?

NICK. To bed.

MARIANNE. We're not done clearing.

NICK. I'll do it in the morning.

MARIANNE. You'll help me do it now.

NICK. I'll do whatever the fuck I want. I'm sleeping in the spare room.

MARIANNE. Edgar?

NICK. Just leave me alone!

> NICK *turns and treads heavily towards the door. At the door he silently takes off his shoes and tiptoes back to her. They kiss.* NICK *helps* MARIANNE *onto the floor. They have to make every move in absolute silence; it's incredibly difficult.* MARIANNE *reaches out to hold a chair leg. The chair moves. They stop and then continue. Suddenly we hear a sound. They stop in alarm. Was that just the boiler? They hear the sound again. They sit upright. They can't continue. They look at one another in defeat.* NICK *quietly stands. Before leaving, he kisses her hand or forehead. He tiptoes to the door and leaves.*

Scene Seven

A meeting place.

NICK, MARIANNE *and* MILLER.

MARIANNE. It feels like we're actually having a dialogue now. Doesn't it?

NICK. Yes, definitely.

MARIANNE. There's a definite fluidity.

NICK. Right.

MARIANNE. A real back and forth.

NICK. A rally.

MARIANNE. A rally, exactly. There's a natural rhythm
developing.

NICK. Very natural.

MARIANNE. And you're really getting to grips with the
rhythm. Edgar's speech pattern, I think you really understand
it now.

NICK. I feel like I understand it.

MARIANNE. You do, it feels very honest.

NICK. Thank you.

MARIANNE. It just feels like there's been a very real shift.

NICK. Yes.

MARIANNE. And we're ready. We're ready to go off script.

Beat.

MILLER. Go on.

NICK. It's chaos out there. They'll have all their manpower on
the protests, not the surveillance. They don't have time to
listen to us any more. Besides, this is, this is about
practicality. I'm trying to handle volatile liquids and at the
same time reading from a sheet of paper. I mean, it's a
health-and-safety issue if nothing else.

MARIANNE. If we could stand where we want, and say what
we want –

NICK. Say what we needed to say then I could be more
efficient.

MILLER. Efficient?

NICK. I could do it in half the time if I didn't have to maintain
an argument, you see what I'm saying?

MARIANNE. If we're expected to stand either side of the room
shouting at each other, how can I help him?

NICK. Exactly. The component parts, they're very small.

MARIANNE. I've got smaller hands.

NICK. We need the opportunity to be... We need...

MARIANNE. We need proximity.

MILLER. Is that right?

NICK. Surely they can be over it by now?

MARIANNE. You said yourself it was only temporary.

MILLER. Did I?

NICK. Yes.

MARIANNE. This dynamic isn't sustainable. I mean, she's become a walking cash machine; she's an attractive package. If this relationship's going to work long term he has to match that at the very least, or, I don't know, she'll have an affair. Isn't it time Edgar got a promotion?

NICK. Yeah.

MARIANNE. Or why doesn't he inherit some money or something? Doesn't he have rich relatives or something?

NICK. Just something to restore the balance.

MARIANNE. Yeah, just...

NICK. Bring them back in line.

MARIANNE. Don't you think?

    Beat.

MILLER. You called me all the way out here to ask if you could go off script?

NICK. We thought –

MILLER. There's nothing wrong? Nothing's broken?

NICK. No...

MILLER. You're not missing something; you've got enough materials?

NICK. No, it's –

MILLER. You don't have enough?

NICK. No, we do, I –

MILLER. You do?

NICK. Yes, everything's fine.

MILLER. Everything's fine?

NICK. Yes.

MILLER. Good, then get back to work.

    MILLER *turns to leave.*

NICK. When are we going? You can't just not tell us.

MILLER. You're not.

NICK. What?

MILLER. You're not going.

MARIANNE. What d'you mean, we're not going?

MILLER. You're staying in that house.

MARIANNE. What?

NICK. On whose authority?

MILLER. Mine. (*Referring to their double act.*) Whatever this is, I don't want it in the field.

MARIANNE. What d'you mean by –

MILLER. It's decided.

NICK. Anna and Tim came to ours last night; they were all over the place. It's one thing to watch me build it; it's another thing to detonate it. You need a safe pair of hands out there.

MILLER. It's decided.

NICK. Are you serious?

MILLER. Our leader has been arrested on trumped-up charges and we've no one to replace him. Am I serious about keeping my technicians from going to jail as well? Yes, I am. That is unless you want the next seven years to continue like this, people turning up with bullets in the neck. We need to protect our houses. And we need to protect our technicians.

NICK. I'm not even that, am I? I'm a glorified fucking janitor.

MILLER. I can't fight you every time we meet; a little trust would be nice. I know you have a complicated relationship with trust. You're a defector. You can't open a bank account. You can't rent a house, nothing. Edgar and Annabel are your bread and butter, no?

NICK *doesn't respond.*

MARIANNE. When's it going to happen?

MILLER. I can't tell you.

NICK. A little trust would be nice.

MILLER. If anything were to happen, I don't want you implicating yourselves or the house. You'll know when it's done. Don't call me out here again. If and when it's the right time to come off script, I will let you know. We committed to the 'disparate earnings' story, you can't just change your mind; it has to play itself out in real time.

MILLER *exits.*

Scene Eight

EDGAR *and* ANNABEL*'s kitchen.*

NICK *sits at the table with a saucepan of cooked potatoes. He vigorously mashes them. He exerts all his frustrations on them. At one point he stops, defeated, before taking up the potato masher once more and continuing.*

A key is heard in the lock and MARIANNE *returns home.*
NICK *is too angry to engage with her; he continues to mash.*
MARIANNE *stares at him. He reads from the script at his side.*

NICK. I'm just reheating the casserole. I've tried my best, but I'm sure you'll want to mash the potatoes a second time to make sure there are no lumps. I know how much it upsets you when...

MARIANNE *waves her hand to attract his attention. She presses a finger to her lips to shush him. She produces two brand-new scripts from her handbag, one of which she offers to him. He takes it. She urges him to read. Unless stated otherwise they both read from the new scripts.*

I added some kidney beans to the casserole; I'm just reheating it now.

MARIANNE *gestures for him to skip a line or two.*

MARIANNE (*unscripted*). Don't worry about the mashed potatoes.

NICK (*finding the line*). And I used the last of the broccoli.

MARIANNE. Great.

NICK *looks at her, confused;* MARIANNE *gestures for him to continue.*

NICK. What took you so long?

MARIANNE. There were station closures.

NICK. The dinner's almost ruined.

MARIANNE. Edgar, haven't you seen the news?

NICK. No, I was cooking.

MARIANNE. Somebody tried to blow up the Ministry of Defence. It was on the news just now in the gym. Apparently the police foiled a massive, coordinated attack in the nick of time. There were six of them. They targeted the Ministry of Defence. They're saying all the suspects have been arrested. All of them. They are confident there will be no more arrests.

The devices were found and diffused after one of the suspects gave away the locations. Two of them were shot while trying to escape. A man and woman. They didn't give any names. Edgar, can you believe it? I can't. I can't believe they came so close.

NICK *grabs his shoulder bag and begins to fill it.*
MARIANNE *pursues him trying desperately to communicate the upcoming message.*

I expect it will drive the rebels underground. I expect they'll be fleeing the country. Cowards. Not me. Not us. Nobody is going to drive us out of our house. Our house is the most precious thing we have. We're safe here. Here we are safe.

NICK *comes to a stop.* MARIANNE *urges him to read. She shakes his script at him.*

Edgar? Days like this make me grateful for what we have. Let's eat our casserole. Come on. You've done such a good job on this mashed potato. Not a single lump. You know how upset it makes me? Edgar? You know how –

NICK (*forcing himself to read*). I know how upset it makes you.

MARIANNE. Yes.

NICK. I'm so glad you're okay.

MARIANNE. Can you imagine if...?

NICK. Yes, that would have been a disaster.

MARIANNE. Awful.

NICK. I hope they lock them up and throw away the key.

NICK *lowers his script in disgust;* MARIANNE *implores him to continue.*

The man who shot those terrorists; I'd like to shake his hand.

MARIANNE. I'd like to shake it too.

NICK. I'd like to thank him. All of them. I'd like to thank them all for the great job they are doing in protecting our country.

Protecting us from criminals. Hateful criminal scum. I hope they get what's coming to them. If anything, this is a timely reminder that we are at war with the kinds of people who will use any means to destroy our nation's love of… (*Cannot bring himself to say the words*.) Our nation's love of… No.

NICK *throws down his script in disgust*.

MARIANNE. Edgar?

NICK. No.

MARIANNE. Edgar, finish what you were saying?

NICK. No.

MARIANNE (*pressing the script on him*). Finish what you were saying: 'Our nation's love –

NICK. Stop it.

MARIANNE. – of freedom and democracy.'

NICK. Stop it. STOP PUTTING WORDS IN MY MOUTH!

NICK *storms from the room*.

Scene Nine

EDGAR *and* ANNABEL*'s kitchen*.

MARIANNE *stands at the kitchen counter decanting pasta from a packet into an airtight jar. She writes on the label as she reads from her script*.

MARIANNE. Fuselli. Wholewheat. Organic.

She reaches for a second packet of pasta and a second jar.

The door opens and ANTHONY, *a man closely resembling* NICK, *enters wearing a raincoat. He carries an umbrella, two bound documents and a plastic shopping bag.*

ANTHONY. Hi, honey. I'm home.

MARIANNE (*turning to him*). Hi, darling.

MARIANNE *freezes. She stares at him. He meets her gaze.*

ANTHONY. It's raining again. (*Beat.*) There's nothing more depressing than being rained on, is there? Just brings down your whole day.

ANTHONY *extends an arm to offer* MARIANNE *a new script. She doesn't take it.*

I'm sorry I'm late. But I had to stand in a doorway for ten minutes. And I'm sorry about yesterday too; for losing my rag. I'm a dick. I didn't mean to accuse you of putting words in my mouth. That's ridiculous. (*With emphasis.*) I'm sorry.

ANTHONY *presses the script on her.* MARIANNE *begins to shake her head.*

So. How was your day?

ANTHONY *opens her script to the right page and holds it up for her; he points to her line.* MARIANNE *cannot speak.*

(*Improvising around her lines.*) Did you get some more recycling bags? You know how you said you'd get some more recycling bags?

Beat.

Because you hate throwing all that plastic away. Yes?

MARIANNE. No.

ANTHONY. Yes you did.

MARIANNE. No.

ANTHONY (*pressing the script on her*). You did, Annabel, why wouldn't you get recycling bags?

MARIANNE. Because it's bullshit.

ANTHONY. Annabel…?

MARIANNE (*pushing the script away*). Recycling is bullshit.

ANTHONY. Annabel…

MARIANNE. Why, why spend my time sorting through rubbish and, and washing out the inside of mayonnaise jars when, when –

ANTHONY. Don't be silly, Annabel.

MARIANNE. Really the only efficient recyclable is, is aluminium.

ANTHONY. Annabel, that's not what you think.

ANTHONY *has pursued* MARIANNE *to the sink; he tries to take hold of her.*

MARIANNE. I think recycling is one of the most wasteful fucking –

ANTHONY *puts a hand over her mouth.* MARIANNE *reaches for a kitchen knife from the sink and, wrapping her fist around it, pulls it clean through her skin. She lets out a scream. She drops the knife and clutches her palm; blood runs down her arm. She howls in pain.*

ANTHONY. Oh my God!

MARIANNE *slumps;* ANTHONY *steadies her.*

(*Unscripted.*) Annabel, oh dear, what have you done? (*Taking hold of her hand.*) Let me see? What is it? Oh, it's just a little cut.

The blood pours thick and fast.

You've just nicked yourself with the knife, that's all, no big deal.

MARIANNE *heaves against the pain.*

Don't be squeamish, sweetheart; it's only tiny. No!

He confiscates the knife and thrusts the script into her hand; he returns to his own script.

What do you say we order a takeaway? I can't be bothered cooking, can you? My treat. Whatever you fancy, it's on me.

(*With emphasis.*) I want to make it up to you. It's just us. Edgar and Annabel. For ever.

MARIANNE *is quiet.*

Let's order a takeaway, okay? Yes?

MARIANNE *nods.*

Okay?

MARIANNE. Yes.

ANTHONY. Okay, there you go. Look at you, you're okay. Aren't you, you're okay? So what are you having? Sweet and sour beef?

Beat.

MARIANNE. Lemon chicken.

Scene Ten

A meeting place.

MARIANNE *and* MILLER, *alone.*

MILLER. He'd been drinking. From what I can tell, after he left for work in the morning, he went straight to the pub and spent the entire day drinking himself into a state. By the time they apprehended him he could hardly stand. Fortunately they didn't link him to the bomb plot; he was identified as a defector. He's being held on a charge of defection, nothing more.

MARIANNE. He didn't drink.

MILLER. Sorry?

MARIANNE. He wasn't a drinker.

MILLER. What you need to understand about him is that he has
a history. His choice to defect: not so much about ideology,
more in fear of disciplinary action.

MARIANNE. How… I'm sorry, how did the police get
involved?

MILLER. The army, he was picked up by the army.

MARIANNE. How would they know he's a defector?

MILLER. Somebody must have recognised him.

MARIANNE. He doesn't see anyone he used to know.

MILLER. Maybe it was someone from out of town.

MARIANNE. Who happened to be in the same pub?

MILLER. Presumably.

Beat.

Look, to be honest, this works out better for us. We took a
risk when we allowed him on board and the risk backfired,
I'll be the first to admit that. You were right all along; he
wasn't a good match. He was fuelled by aggression and
high-fructose corn syrup; he's better off back in army.

MARIANNE. You know what they do to defectors.

MILLER. He wasn't capable of delivering the results we need.
And right now, incompatibility is not an option.

Pause.

He was a liability; I mean, look how he's affected you.
Before he came along you'd never have lost your temper,
would you? You and Carl were perfect on script and off.
You'd never have argued about recycling.

MARIANNE. No.

MILLER. Edgar and Annabel would never argue about recycling.

MARIANNE. No, course not.

MILLER. Recycling is integral to who they are as a couple and what they tell themselves they stand for. They don't question the economics. It's not in their nature.

MARIANNE. No, no, of course.

MILLER. That's what makes Edgar and Annabel the perfect cover.

MARIANNE. Right.

MILLER. They don't question their choices; they just choose them. And they continue to choose them even when they are not economically sustainable because they know in the end their parents will always bail them out. Right?

MARIANNE. Right. Sure.

ANTHONY *enters*.

MILLER. Were you followed?

ANTHONY. No.

MILLER. How d'you get on?

ANTHONY *passes him some documents*.

ANTHONY. We're applying for voluntary strike-off on grounds of retirement. I've earmarked where I need a signature.

MILLER *takes the documents*.

I need signatures from both directors.

MILLER. We can close The Granary?

ANTHONY. There was no outstanding trading debt.

MILLER. Good.

ANTHONY. But we first we have to sell Bickley Street. The business owns the property. It's not a problem. If we close everything at once we might get unwanted attention. But we need to do it before they pick up the trail.

MARIANNE. Why are you closing everything?

ANTHONY. We're in retreat; we've got to scale back to almost nothing. Everything's under suspicion now. The best we can hope for is that we emerge out the other side of this with at least something of the resistance still intact. A couple of the other houses are looking vulnerable, Edgar and Annabel's is safe as far as we know. It's our best bet.

MILLER. Anthony's aware of the need to provide the house with maximum protection. He's agreed to stay on script. I want you to help him revise, take every opportunity you get. You're comfortable with staying on script?

MARIANNE. Of course.

MILLER. Not long ago you were eager to come off. And I can't accommodate anyone's personal preferences.

MARIANNE. I wouldn't ask you to.

MILLER. You have in the past.

MARIANNE. For the sake of the project.

MILLER. The project?

MARIANNE. Yes, I was trying to help.

MILLER. Who?

MARIANNE. Edgar and Annabel. It was for their benefit.

MILLER. It was?

MARIANNE. Yes, I don't need you to accommodate… I'm fine. I'm fine.

MILLER. I don't care if you're fine. It's the relationship that's important, not you. Not me. None of us. If we are to stand a chance of succeeding, Edgar and Annabel need to survive us all.

MARIANNE (*nodding*). Sure, yes. Absolutely.

MILLER. Good. And good luck. (*Turning to go, but stopping short.*) I'm sorry, have you been able to introduce your-selves? Anthony, Marianne.

ANTHONY *extends a hand to* MARIANNE; *she shakes it.*

ANTHONY. Hi.

MARIANNE. Hi, good to meet you.

ANTHONY. And you.

As MARIANNE *extends her arm her sleeve rises to reveal the bandage on her hand.*

MILLER (*noticing the bandage*). What's that? On your hand?

MARIANNE. Nothing.

MILLER. You cut yourself?

MARIANNE. It's nothing.

MILLER. Did you cut yourself?

MARIANNE. I… Yes, it was… On the… An accident, it's nothing.

MILLER *looks to* ANTHONY.

MILLER. Is there a problem?

MARIANNE. Of course there's not a problem. You don't need to question me. How can you question me? Carl, Nick, they gave themselves away; I'm still here. Don't punish me cos they were a pair of amateurs. I'm still here. How can you question me? I've been doing this since the beginning. And what, just because I slip with a knife, suddenly I'm some deranged woman, some kind of mental patient? Suddenly I'm a crazy bitch? I don't think so. I know what I'm doing, thank you. I'm giving everything I've got, every day, every night of my life, until, until I don't know where she ends and I begin. And that's fine, fucking fine, because, because I'm a fucking professional!

Scene Eleven

EDGAR *and* ANNABEL'*s kitchen.*

ANTHONY *chops vegetables on the work surface. He hums contentedly to himself. The key is heard in the lock.*

The door opens and CLAIRE, *a woman closely resembling* MARIANNE, *enters. She wears a raincoat and carries two bound documents and a plastic shopping bag.*

CLARIE. Hi, darling...

    ANTHONY *turns to see her. He freezes. He stares at her.*

    Something smells delicious.

    Beat.

    Is that chicken?

    Beat.

    Is that chicken?

    Beat.

    (*Offering him a new script.*) Chicken?

ANTHONY. Chicken.

CLAIRE. Thought so. Smells delicious.

    They stare at one another.

    The End.

THE SWAN

DC Moore

DC Moore's previous plays include *Alaska* (Royal Court); *Honest* (Royal & Derngate, Northampton; transferred to the Edinburgh Fringe Festival and later the Queen's Head pub in London); *The Empire* (a co-production between the Royal Court and Theatre Royal, Plymouth); and *Town* (Royal & Derngate). In 2008 he won the inaugural Tom Erhardt Award for promising playwrights. *The Empire* won the TMA Award for Best Touring Production, was nominated for an Olivier Award for Outstanding Achievement in an Affiliate Theatre and led to him being nominated for the Evening Standard Award for Most Promising Playwright. He is currently the Pearson Resident Playwright at the Royal Court.

Characters

GRACE
JIM
RUSSELL
DENISE
BRADWELL
AMY
CHRISTINE

The Prologue

1956. A pub in Lambeth, South London; most of which is in darkness. The lights are focused on GRACE, *singing 'Just Walkin' in the Rain' by Johnny Ray. She is pregnant. Drinking. And smoking.*

The Play

Darkness. The sound of rain. A small amount at first; then heavier; then a sudden torrent, which hits the roof of the pub with a pounding, violent force.

Eventually the rain fades. Then there is light on:

Summer, 2011. A Saturday, early afternoon.

We are in the same pub in South London; we can immediately tell it's the sort of pub that – these days – doesn't attract much passing custom. A few tables have been hastily pushed together and are covered with food, all of which is wrapped in cling-film/kitchen foil or in Tupperware. However, on those tables which have not been moved/covered in food, are some near-empty pint glasses and crisp packets; detritus from the previous evening which gives the pub a bit of a Marie Celeste *feel.*

We can see: the doors to the toilets; a space that leads behind the bar (to a back room and rooms upstairs); and the double door entrance/exit of the pub.

There is a jukebox, which might date back to the fifties but could just be one of those square, unobtrusive, wall-mounted modern ones.

One of the double doors opens. Enter JIM, *who is wearing a black suit and white shirt with his collar open: he wears it well.* JIM *is smoking, so he stays in the doorway rather than coming into the pub. He peers in, whilst wedging himself against the open door (to stop it closing on him) and holding the fag out behind the closed door (in order to limit how much smoke seeps into the pub). We can tell from* JIM *(who is a little bit wet) and what we can see outside (some dripping water, etc.) that the rain has only recently stopped. (Note: during the following,* JIM *occasionally looks back over his shoulder/outside to see what the state of the weather is.)*

JIM. Nick, where are ya, mate?

> JIM *pushes himself up on his heels, trying to see if Nick is behind the bar: he isn't.*

> JIM *takes a drag on the fag. Trying to be conscientious and keep smoke out of the pub, he then moves the fag back behind the closed door but – near simultaneously – he exhales whilst facing into the pub. Smoke pours into the room.*

> *Fuck.*

> JIM *tries to waft the smoke back outside the pub with his free hand. Does this until he's happy he's had a good waft at it. He might even kick at it a bit.*

> JIM *looks around the pub and tries to listen as to whether Nick is making any sort of sound anywhere.*

> *Nicholas?* You having a shit? It's alright, sir, we're all friends, we all defecate, dunt we? Well, I do, all the time! *The amount of shit that comes out my arse!*

> *No response.*

> (Fuck sake.) *NICKY! NICK SON!* Can you hear me? You out back? Or are you upstairs having a? On the? *Are ya?*

> *No response.*

> JIM *takes another drag. Gets it right this time and blows the smoke outside.*

JIM *looks at his fag: he doesn't want to throw it away, as there's too much left of it.*

Nicholas, you great cunt, I want serving!

No response.

You bought this on yourself, Nick. I'm coming in, all guns blazing. The fucking. Alamo.

JIM *inhales and then enters the pub. As he comes in, he swivels his head/body around to blow the smoke around as much as possible in every direction. After he runs out of breath, he comes to a standstill near the middle of the room.*

Serves you right!

JIM *gets his breath back a bit/coughs. Then looks momentarily around the pub, almost as if he's looking at it for the first time.*

A moment of silence during which a sense of unease/concern crosses his face. Not just from being a bit breathless.

He then takes a drag and exhales, his head facing down.

An extended moment of complete stillness and quiet.

Oh dear, Jim.

JIM *suddenly snaps out of it, by making some sort of clicky gesture, clap of his hands or double-slap of his own body. He heads straight behind the bar.*

My goodness, it's Guinness. My Guinness, it's goodness. Guinny goody, goody good, boody boody bardy bardy. Baaaaaaah.

JIM *shakes his head/exhales/yawns at his own nonsense. He finds a glass from above him on the shelf and then starts to pour himself a Guinness (which means he has to keep the fag in his mouth whilst he does this).*

I'll invoice ya for this! I will. Time. Fucking. Rendered.

Starting to be genuinely a bit concerned/annoyed, JIM *stops the tap, leaves the semi-poured Guinness, and leans behind the door/space that leads back behind the bar (and up to rooms/space above the pub). Takes a drag. Listens. Exhales.*

NICK, I'M GONNA STEAL ALL YOUR ALCOHOL AND ALL YOUR MONEY, DO A SHIT ON THE BAR, WIDDLE EVERYWHERE AND *THEN* I'M GONNA *BURN THE WHOLE FUCKING BUILDING DOWN*! IT'LL BE LIKE GROUND ZERO! BUT IN LAMBETH!

No response.

AND I'M SMOKING!

No response.

JIM *gives up. He goes back to the bar, takes out a shot glass to use as an ashtray and finishes pouring the Guinness. He then takes out his wallet. However, the till is a bit intimidating to work.* JIM *tries pushing some buttons. It doesn't do anything. He stabs at it with his fingers but still no joy. He tries pushing at the drawer but it won't open. He gives it a hefty punch/whack.*

(*To Nick, raising his voice.*) I haven't got any change, Nick! I can't open the fucking! Can I?

No response.

You silent… cunt.

No response.

Again, a moment of darkness crosses JIM*'s face. He's thinking about something else. He puts the wallet away. Sighs.*

They all are.

JIM *takes a drag and has a sip of Guinness before taking out an iPhone, which has a cracked screen but still works. Looks at it. He 'slides to unlock' and then scrolls through some text messages, shaking his head slightly as he does so. Reads some text messages and then looks at an attached photo, which we can't really see. (Note: we might get the sense that*

JIM *isn't exactly au fait with the phone but he is just about able to work it.*)

JIM *turns the phone over in his hands, so that the screen is facing away from him. However, after a pause, he then flips the screen around, looks at it again intently, shaking his head slightly and closes his eyes.*

Enter RUSSELL, *who is carrying a newspaper:* The Times.

RUSSELL (*slightly surprised*)....Mr Thomas?

JIM. Mr Downing.

RUSSELL. Have you bought the place?

JIM. Yeah, I'm just on my fucking BlackBerry to my broker in Shanghai, liquidate some fucking. Gold reserves.

RUSSELL. That's an iPhone.

JIM. No, it's a new hybrid: an I.Berry.

RUSSELL. Not a, BlackPhone?

JIM. No. (Racist.)

RUSSELL. Seriously, that's a bit fangled for you, isn't it?

JIM....yeah – no – well, yeah, but it was just like a fucking like present from...

JIM *puts the iPhone away.*

...someone.

RUSSELL. Right.

JIM *shrugs/half-smiles.*

RUSSELL *shrugs/half-smiles back.*

JIM. So, were you out in it? Colossal, wun it?

RUSSELL. I was inside, waiting for it to stop. You?

JIM. Got caught in the last of it, not too bad.

RUSSELL *nods.*

JIM *nods.*

RUSSELL. And where is Nick?

JIM *shrugs*.

JIM. Position was vacant when I come in, so just like helping myself.

RUSSELL. Oh. (*Gesturing upstairs*.) So, is he?

JIM. I imagine.

RUSSELL (*doing a little typing gesture to suggest a keyboard*). On his?

JIM. Probably.

RUSSELL. Oh dear.

JIM. Yeah.

RUSSELL. Well he's certainly found a rhythm.

JIM. That is a very nice way of putting it, Mr Downing.

RUSSELL. The consolations of the flesh.

JIM. Yeah. And three-way anal.

RUSSELL *coughs/nods*.

RUSSELL (*referring to the food*). So what's all the, er…?

JIM. Oh yeah. It's. Today.

RUSSELL. What?

JIM. Funeral.

RUSSELL.…of course.

JIM. So just a little like do. Like an after thing here, they're having. We're having. Eating, drinking and fucking. Merriment. Like Brannigans.

RUSSELL. Well then, I should probably…

JIM. No, fuck off, stay, have a drink.

RUSSELL. You're sure that I wouldn't be…?

JIM. *No*, you knew him. (Sort of.) He'd want you to have a drink.

RUSSELL. Would he?

JIM. Course he would, he was an alcoholic.

RUSSELL. Right.

JIM (*looking briefly at his watch*). And we probably got about an hour or so left till they all get here, so. Please. Please.

RUSSELL. Then I will then, thank you.

JIM. What?

RUSSELL. Um, half a Foster's top, a dash of lime, slice of lemon and some scented Lebanese ice.

JIM. *Fuck off!*

RUSSELL *smiles*.

RUSSELL. John Smith's please, Mr Thomas.

JIM (*starting to pour the drink*). Wanker.

RUSSELL. Yeah.

RUSSELL *watches him pour.*

You seem in good... spirit. Considering.

JIM....

RUSSELL. I don't mean anything by that, or.

JIM. No.

RUSSELL. I'm not...

JIM. I know.

RUSSELL. We all have our own ways of...

JIM. Yeah yeah.

RUSSELL. Don't we?

JIM *nods*.

JIM. 'Parently.

> JIM *finishes pouring and places the drink on the bar.*

> That's on the house. (*Referring to the till.*) At least till we work out how that little cuntknocker works.

> RUSSELL *nods and takes the drink.*

RUSSELL. Thank you.

> JIM *studies* RUSSELL *as he takes a sip.*

JIM. You know, this is the probably the first time we've been alone together.

RUSSELL. Is it?

JIM. I reckon.

RUSSELL. You're not going to make a pass at me, are you?

JIM. No. (Bender.) Just. I never asked you. Serious fucking question.

RUSSELL. Please.

JIM. Why do you drink in here?

RUSSELL. Well, I live round the corner.

JIM. Yeah but, I mean, like, I was born in this fucking pub. Well, not really but her waters broke over there somewhere. My dear old mum – Grace – bless her. She always used to sing in here – lovely fucking voice she had and she'd get everyone to fucking like, join in, you know, all round the pub – and one night – right? – after she was done. Singing. I come along.

RUSSELL. I know.

JIM. (Gush.) How do ya?

RUSSELL. Because you always get drunk and tell everyone.

JIM. Right. Well. From that fucking point on, mate, I was pretty much brought up in here. My dad had fucked the fuck off to Nowheresville before I was even born, so she'd bring me in

here all the time. This place was pretty much my fucking.
Nursery. School. Uni. (Well, polytechnic.) Everything you
could do. Kiss girls. Fight men. Be sick. A lot. Pool, when
we had one. I've done it all, in here. (*A brief pause.*) I mean,
Mum, she was a beautiful woman and I watched her... get
old in here, you know?

RUSSELL. Yeah.

A pause.

JIM. So, in every conceivable fucking sense: this is my local.

RUSSELL. Right.

JIM. Right. But even I – right? – I have to fucking wonder. I do.
'Why do I still come here?'

RUSSELL. Lots of reasons.

JIM. Like – honestly – two nights ago, I sat there and listened to
Mad Tommy tell me in unrelentingly extravagant detail
about the time he kicked a dog to death coz it pissed on a car.

RUSSELL. Right.

JIM. It weren't even his.

RUSSELL. The dog or the car?

JIM. Either. And that's before we get on to what he's done to
actual fucking humans, you know?

RUSSELL. Okay, yeah. Tommy is a bit... out on a limb.

JIM. Yeah, and he ain't alone in here, these days. So maybe
they're right, sell it all off.

RUSSELL. How long till the sale goes through?

JIM. Few weeks, according to Nick. Paperwork. Legal stuff.
Finalities.

RUSSELL *nods.*

RUSSELL. Someone else could buy it, maybe.

JIM. They have. Fucking. Developers.

RUSSELL. No. Another brewery. Locals.

JIM. What, like fucking Big Society?

RUSSELL. Well, maybe not quite like that but...

JIM. Fuck all that, brewery have had planning permission, *years*. Just been waiting for takings to. (*Gestures 'plummet' and makes an appropriate sound.*) And they have, so we're – officially – 'not fucking viable'.

RUSSELL. So this will all be flats.

JIM nods.

JIM. Just think, where I'm stood right now will be someone's fucking. Living room. Or toilet.

RUSSELL. Yeah.

JIM. They could be having a horrible future poo right where I'm standing.

RUSSELL. Possibly.

JIM. Which would be fucking typical, by the way.

RUSSELL. It's all rather sad, really.

JIM. I dunno, mate – like I say – maybe it's a fucking like. Blessing. (*Pause.*) Anyway, back to the original fucking question.

RUSSELL. Which was?

A brief pause as JIM remembers it.

JIM. Yeah. Why do you drink in here?

RUSSELL. Well...

JIM. Coz you're an upstanding cunt of the fucking realmy cunt, intya?

RUSSELL. That is one way of summarising my.

JIM. And this place ain't exactly the Garrick now, is it?

RUSSELL. No.

JIM. So enlighten me, oh Zen Buddha master.

RUSSELL. Well, Mr Thomas. Do you happen to see my wife on the premises?

JIM. No.

RUSSELL. And have you *ever* seen my wife on the premises?

JIM. No.

RUSSELL. Have you, in fact, any idea what she looks or sounds like?

JIM. No.

RUSSELL. And have you ever seen me looking concerned in any way that my wife might soon suddenly arrive on the premises?

JIM. No.

RUSSELL. Quod erat demonstrandum.

JIM. Right.

RUSSELL. (Q.E.D.)

JIM. (Yeah.)

RUSSELL. Without the last ten years, hiding in here, I imagine I'd be dead, divorced, or in prison. Seriously, I probably would have killed her by now. And then myself, afterwards.

A pause.

JIM. Oh.

JIM *nods.*

RUSSELL. Yeah. So when it does close. God help me. And her. But: 'Do not underestimate the determination of a quiet man.'

JIM. IDS.

RUSSELL *nods.*

RUSSELL. 2002 conference. I was there. Possibly the worst speech ever given by a conscious biped. Or a leader of the Conservative Party.

JIM. Yeah, he was a cunt, wun he?

RUSSELL. Still is.

JIM. You know my favourite saying, like life-quote 'n' that?

RUSSELL *shakes his head.*

My big brother – Teddy – told me when I was like fifteen fourteen. Pretty much the last thing he said to me.

RUSSELL.…?

JIM. 'If you won't eat it, don't fuck it.'

RUSSELL.…

JIM *nods.*

JIM. It means if you wouldn't go down on her.

RUSSELL. Yeah, I think we caught the general gist of the.

JIM. Coz if you won't put your mush in – all up amongst it, nose in ra ra ra, fully committed, fucking, kamikaze – you probably shouldn't shove your conkers up.

RUSSELL. No.

JIM. 'Coz there be demons.'

RUSSELL. Yeah. No. Well, something to… To mull, anyway. Think I might – actually – retire to the, er.

JIM. Oh yeah, me going on.

RUSSELL. No no, I just have a vicious little bastard of a crossword to, er.

JIM. Coolio. Yeah.

RUSSELL. Yeah.

JIM. You have it, son. *Smash it.*

RUSSELL *nods.*

RUSSELL. I will, yeah. (*Doing his best Cockney, with a fist motion.*) 'Yeah.'

JIM *smiles/laughs*. RUSSELL *smiles back, slightly apologetically*.

Sorry, I won't ever do that again.

JIM. No, please do, sir.

RUSSELL *smiles/shakes his head then goes to move towards the corner, whilst taking a sip, but about halfway he stops, turns*.

RUSSELL (*still smiling*). And erm, an hour, you said?

JIM. What?

RUSSELL. You said they won't all be here for another hour.

JIM. Yeah.

RUSSELL. But if you're here, why aren't they? Sorry if that's a rude question, or...

JIM. No, no, they're just all at the... Like, they're all *at* the... the service. It's happening now, like.

RUSSELL. Right, so you didn't...?

JIM. No.

RUSSELL.... go?

JIM. Yeah. No.

RUSSELL *nods*.

RUSSELL. Right. Can I ask, why?

JIM. Yeah.

RUSSELL. Why?

JIM....

A pause.

JIM *shrugs*.

Who knows why we do what we do, eh? Fucking... mystery, ain't it?

RUSSELL. Sometimes.

JIM. Human nature, yeah. Nuts.

RUSSELL *nods*.

JIM *nods*.

A pause.

RUSSELL. Anyway, to Michael.

JIM....yeah.

JIM *nods*.

RUSSELL *toasts his drink*.

JIM *tentatively raises his glass*.

RUSSELL. May he find. Peace, if that's the right word.

JIM....

RUSSELL. Finally.

JIM *nods*.

RUSSELL *and* JIM *drink a toast*.

RUSSELL *retreats to a corner, where he starts on a crossword*. JIM *exhales deeply*.

A phone starts to ring.

JIM. Oh Jesus.

A pause.

JIM *takes out his iPhone but it's not the right phone. Annoyed and slightly flustered (between his fag, pint and two phones), JIM puts the iPhone down somewhere behind the bar. He then takes out a different phone: a very basic but durable little brick of a Nokia. He goes to answer but then looks at the screen. He closes his eyes, hoping it will make it go away. Shakes his head a bit*.

However, unseen by JIM, DENISE – dressed in black, wearing a long coat – is in the doorway with her phone in her hand.

DENISE. Are you gonna answer?

JIM *opens his eyes. Looks at her.*

JIM. Maybe.

DENISE *hangs up, puts the phone away. Inspects* JIM, *who puts his Nokia away.*

DENISE. I thought you would be.

JIM. What?

DENISE. Here.

JIM. Sherlock.

DENISE. You promised.

JIM. Yeah.

DENISE. Didn't ya?

JIM. Denise.

A brief pause.

DENISE. How can you lie, like that?

JIM. I didn't lie. Exactly.

DENISE. May as well.

JIM. I didn't, I just changed my...

DENISE. Don't lie about not lying.

JIM *sighs. Nods. Inspects* DENISE.

JIM. So what, has it finished early then?

DENISE *shakes her head.*

So how come you're...?

DENISE. I didn't stay.

JIM (*half-joking*). What, you walk out in the middle of it?

DENISE. Sort of.

A brief pause.

JIM. Are you are you fucking joking me?

DENISE. Yeah, I'm being really funny.

JIM. Fucky... fucky... *fuck, Denis*e. Why d'ya do that for?

DENISE. If you don't have to go, then I don't see why I should stay for the...

JIM. Your mum is gonna rape and kill me, then dig up my corpse, do it again.

DENISE. Yeah.

JIM. Won't she?

DENISE. Yeah.

JIM. Coz she'll blame me for you leaving.

DENISE *nods*.

DENISE. Guess so.

JIM. Oh, thank you very much.

DENISE. But I think she would have... done all that to you anyway, for not turning up.

JIM. You're right, Watson. Elementary. Fucking... (*A brief pause*.) So, did I miss much?

DENISE. Not really.

JIM. Hymns 'n' that.

DENISE. Yeah.

JIM. Priest stuff.

DENISE *nods*.

Eulogies.

DENISE. I didn't stay for that. That's all now.

JIM *nods*.

JIM. But you did your reading?

DENISE *shrugs*.

You didn't?

DENISE *shrugs*.

Oh, fuck me, girl. Your mum. Warpath. Me. On the fucking. For.

DENISE. Yeah.

JIM. Christ on a mechanised... fucking, Chinese...

JIM *shakes his head/exhales long and hard*.

Suppose you want a drink then?

DENISE *nods*.

DENISE. Coke.

JIM. Yeah.

JIM *nods, starts to make her a Coke*.

Thin or fat?

DENISE. Fat.

JIM. Sure you don't want like an Irish Coke, or?

DENISE. No.

JIM. Coz I don't wanna drink on me own, do I? (*Referring to* RUSSELL.) Downton Abbey there don't count.

RUSSELL. Pardon?

JIM. Nothing, Mr Downing, shut up.

RUSSELL. Righto.

DENISE. I'm alright, thank you.

JIM. You look. You do, you look. Whimberful.

DENISE. I know.

JIM. It's a made-up word, how d'ya know what it means? Might be horrible.

DENISE. I just do.

JIM. What about me?

DENISE. Yeah yeah, you look good, yeah.

JIM. Thank you, that's very nice of you to say, Denise.

As he says this, JIM *gives her the Coke.*

DENISE *sips at it. Momentarily looks back at the exit/entrance. A similar look of concern (to* JIM*'s) fleetingly crosses her face.*

So we mates then?

DENISE *nods, distracted.*

DENISE. Yeah. We could still go back for the end of the…?

JIM. Fuck off.

DENISE. Yeah, suppose. (*A pause.*) Why do people wear black at funerals?

JIM. Erm.

DENISE. Does it mean death? Or like, regret?

JIM. No.

DENISE. Why then?

JIM. It's just very slimming.

DENISE *smiles a little.*

DENISE. Really?

JIM. Yeah, I mean, day like this you got grief and pain tumbling around inside ya like a spastic in a spin-dryer.

DENISE. Jim.

JIM. What? Then suddenly you're surrounded by all these relatives, old friends; most of whom you don't like trust or respect and who you ain't seen *in fucking years* – for good fucking reason, mostly – and now you gotta talk to 'em like they're the fucking proverbial fucking. Risen from the fucking. So yeah, last thing you wanna be worrying about is whether you look like a fat cunt. Hence. Thus. Ergo. Black.

DENISE. That's actually why?

JIM. Would I lie to you?

DENISE. No.

JIM. I never would. Your mum let you smoke yet?

DENISE. I don't need. Permission.

JIM. You do.

DENISE. I don't.

JIM. Alright: you don't. (But you do.) Anyway, d'ya mind if I smoke in here, then?

DENISE. It's illegal.

JIM (*already lighting up*). So's invading countries, don't stop anyone.

DENISE *scoffs/smiles/shakes her head and watches* JIM *inhale/exhale.*

Sure you don't want a bit o' voddy in it? You can't smell vodka, one of the perks.

DENISE *considers this, briefly looks back to the door.*

DENISE. Okay then.

JIM. Good girl.

JIM *takes the Coke back, tops it up with vodka.*

DENISE. So what, you're the big barman today?

JIM. Na na, it's still Dirty Nick but he ain't surfaced yet.

DENISE. Where is he?

JIM *shrugs a bit and then hands the Coke/vodka back.*

JIM. Two options. The nicer one – unlikely as we live in a cold dark universe – he's playing poker online.

DENISE. What? He's got a pub to run.

JIM. *Yeah*, but he's got this fucking idea in his head now that
   he's gonna become a professional fucking poker player when
   this place closes down. Which is – as ideas go – about as
   sensible as invading Russia during winter, on your own,
   when you're pissed. On gin.

DENISE. What's the other option?

JIM. Well, the more likely scenario, what Mr Downing and I
   would both put rather a lot of fucking money on: he'll be
   knocking one out.

DENISE. What?

JIM. He's unrelenting, honestly, girl. I mean, the day he got that
   broadband connection, a a a light went out in his eyes. Now
   he's just like some fucking junkie: only about the next hit.

DENISE. But of like, porno?

JIM. *Yeah*. And the rest.

DENISE. Like what?

JIM. You don't wanna know.

DENISE. I do.

JIM. You don't. I don't. So I ain't going up there, check on him.

DENISE. Eugh.

JIM. Yeah, Dirty Nick is… He earnt the nickname, let's put it
   that way. Up there's like fucking downtown Bangkok
   crossed with fucking. *Blade Runner*.

   JIM *and* DENISE *share a smile/laugh: she's very used to his
   filthy banter.*

   Though he usually makes sure someone's down here,
   manning the fucking. *Enterprise*. The bridge. One of the
   Polish girls, or. Mad Sally. (Whilst he's at it.) But I suppose
   if they're selling it all off: what's the point? (*Pause*.) So are
   you alright, then?

DENISE. How do you mean?

JIM. 'Bout today 'n' that.

DENISE. Yeah. Yeah. You?

JIM. What?

DENISE. Are you... alright?

JIM. Yeah yeah yeah. Good. Really good.

DENISE. Just that I think normally fathers are meant to go to their own son's funerals.

A brief pause.

JIM. Are they?

DENISE *nods.*

DENISE. I read it somewhere. In *Glamour.*

A little smile from JIM.

JIM. Look, Dee. I know it looks really fucking... Just, funerals and me don't... I mean, it's just bullshit, ain't it? It's all... Just like a fucking... Like. Show.

DENISE. Yeah, but it's a show for God. And your family.

JIM. Yeah, well that's not... not how I see it, is it, darling?

DENISE. But Michael was your own flesh and...

JIM *(losing his temper slightly). I do know. (Calmer.)* Look, it was my decision to make, okay? And I made it. Can you respect that, please?

A brief pause.

DENISE *nods.*

DENISE. Try.

JIM. Thank you. And fuck off anyway, coz you just walked out o' it.

DENISE *(hint of a grin).* Yeah.

JIM. Lecture me, ya cheeky cunt.

DENISE. Yeah.

JIM. 'Language.'

DENISE *nods/smiles*.

DENISE. Yeah.

A brief pause.

JIM. So you got a job yet?

DENISE *shakes her head*.

Still applying?

DENISE. For everything. Everywhere.

JIM. Well, don't worry about it, not your fault, is it?

DENISE. Feels like it.

JIM. Na na, tell ya who's fault it is.

DENISE. Who's that?

JIM. International *laissez-faire* Capitalism.

DENISE. That's not a person.

JIM. *Yeah*, but when I was kid, you couldn't fall over without getting a fucking job. Now, you've gotta get a fucking degree and PhD in fucking biophysics to work as third fucking marketing assistant in a leisure centre in Croydon with some randy pug-nosed *twats*.

DENISE (*not a genuine question*). So it would be better if we had International Socialism?

JIM. *No*, because then you'd be the third fucking potato assistant, whatever you did.

DENISE *nods. Smiles*.

DENISE. Would I?

JIM *nods*.

JIM. Yeah.

A brief pause.

DENISE. So how are you gonna say goodbye? To Michael.

JIM. ...Denise.

DENISE. I think you need to. I think you should... like... You know? I think you might be the only person who knew what he really was like. To me. To... Mum.

JIM. Love.

DENISE. I do.

JIM. I know you do but... I just wanna drink. Get through the fucking... Say hello. Make a noise or two. Alright? (*A brief pause.*) Alright?

DENISE. ...

DENISE *nods.*

JIM. And I do wear this suit well, don't I?

DENISE. Yeah.

JIM. Look like Rock Hudson. But straight. Talking of which, how you doing for boys these days?

DENISE. I don't wanna...

JIM. Come on. You can tell me, love.

DENISE. Can I?

JIM. Course.

DENISE *exhales/smiles.*

DENISE. Okay.

A pause as DENISE *gathers her thoughts.*

It all dies.

JIM. What?

RUSSELL *looks up at* DENISE *and watches her throughout the rest of her explanation.*

DENISE. Like. Every time you kiss someone. Or touch them. The first time you do that. With anyone. You make something. Between you.

JIM. Okay.

DENISE. And it has like its own life, you know?

JIM. Think so.

DENISE. But neither of you, can control it, not really. And it gets bigger, stronger, the more time you're with someone. But there's always a point, where it stops, like… getting bigger. Where it starts to, get weak. And then. Collapses. Under its own… You know? (*A brief pause*.) So basically, whenever you kiss someone, you're just creating something –. a sort of life – knowing that one day you're gonna watch it die, in front of you. (*A brief pause*.) And I don't wanna do that no more. I can't.

JIM. Right.

DENISE. You know?

JIM. Jesus H. Corbett, Denise. You're barely out of school uniform, how can you be thinking like that?

DENISE. Coz I've got a brain.

RUSSELL. She's right. She is.

JIM. Earwigging, Mr Downing?

RUSSELL. Sorry, ignore me.

DENISE. It's okay.

RUSSELL. 'Apologies to the House.'

DENISE. No.

JIM. Don't be a fucking poof, mate, it's alright.

RUSSELL. Okay. Sorry for being a. A poof.

JIM. Yeah.

RUSSELL *smiles/raises his eyebrows at* DENISE *before going back to his crossword.*

How did this estate produce you, eh?

DENISE. Magic.

JIM. Must be. Or that fucking school.

DENISE. Jim.

JIM. What?

DENISE. Don't joke about that.

JIM. I didn't.

DENISE. Well, don't.

JIM. I'm not.

DENISE. No, but your tone. Please.

JIM. You got through it though, didn't ya?

DENISE. No. I didn't.

A brief pause.

JIM. Changed since I went there, tell ya. Wanna top-up?

DENISE *nods.*

Course you do.

Suddenly, they hear some stumbling and a series of thuds/thumps in the men's toilets.

Nick? Is that you, mate, you alright?

JIM *has moved round from the bar towards the toilet. The toilet door opens. But it isn't Nick, it's* BRADWELL. *He's an absolute state. He is wearing a suit for the funeral and it has a few inauspicious stains on it. He is wearing one shoe.*

BRADWELL. I don't know what's going on, is it.

A brief pause as JIM *and* DENISE *take him in.*

JIM. How long you been in there?

BRADWELL. I don't know.

JIM. What you been doing?

BRADWELL. I don't know.

DENISE. Are you alright?

A brief pause.

BRADWELL. I don't know.

DENISE (*genuine question, with concern*). Is there anything you do know, Bradwell?

BRADWELL. Yeah, I lost a shoe. (*Referring to the toilet behind him.*) And you don't wanna go in there for like a long long time.

JIM. Fucking hell, what you done?

BRADWELL. A few… Quite a few things actually.

JIM. Like what?

BRADWELL. Like… a mixture, I think. I don't really wanna talk about it.

JIM. Jesus.

BRADWELL. Yeah.

BRADWELL *nods.*

I know. Have you seen any spare shoes in here?

JIM. No, Bradwell.

BRADWELL. Fuck sake.

DENISE. Wondered why you didn't make it.

BRADWELL. Did I miss it then?

DENISE. Yeah.

BRADWELL. Was it any good?

DENISE. Bradwell, it's a funeral.

BRADWELL. Yeah, sorry, yeah.

BRADWELL *nods*.

DENISE. So I take it Amy ain't with you? You said you were gonna bring her.

BRADWELL. Erm… No. No, I didn't invite her in the end, thought it might be a bit weird.

JIM. Who's Amy?

DENISE. His new girl; ain't met her yet but he just keeps talking 'bout her talking 'bout her talking 'bout her.

JIM. Another one? Fuck-a-diddle Bradwell.

BRADWELL *nods*.

JIM. What she like?

BRADWELL. Yeah, I like her, a lot. She's quite moody but I think that's quite sexy actually.

JIM. Well, she's obviously a very lucky girl.

BRADWELL. Do ya think?

A little look/smile between JIM *and* DENISE.

JIM. Absolutely.

BRADWELL. Ah, thank you.

BRADWELL*'s phone starts to ring. It's 'Stompbox (Spor Remix)' by the The Qemists. It's very loud and made worse by the fact that very quickly it gets to the bit that is normally forty-six seconds into the song (where the breakbeat kicks in).*

BRADWELL *is in too delicate a state to handle this. He takes out the phone.*

I don't like it, take it, take it, please.

DENISE *takes the phone. Answers it.*

DENISE. Hello?

DENISE listens to the response.

(*Half-whispering, covering up the phone.*) It's Amy. She's a bit angry.

BRADWELL. Why?

A brief pause.

DENISE (*into the phone*). We're in The Swan. The pub.

BRADWELL. *Fuck.*

DENISE. Just walk directly over the car park, you'll see it.

DENISE listens to the phone briefly.

(*Looking at* BRADWELL.) Yeah, he is a bit.

DENISE hangs up. Hands the phone back to BRADWELL.

She's on her way. She's just at yours.

BRADWELL takes the phone.

BRADWELL. *No.* I can't. *I really can't.*

JIM. Can't what?

BRADWELL. …anything. I like her too much to let her see me all like… We're at that stage you, know? Like, I barely swear in front of her, I don't cum too soon. Nothing.

JIM. Gentleman.

BRADWELL. Yeah, I know.

BRADWELL is a bit breathless/nauseous.

JIM. Would some food help?

BRADWELL. No.

JIM. How about a drink?

BRADWELL. Maybe.

JIM. It's free.

BRADWELL. Go on then.

JIM moves back round behind the bar.

JIM (*as he moves*). Hair o' the cunt.

BRADWELL unsteadily approaches the bar.

BRADWELL (*without looking at* RUSSELL, *just giving a vague wave in his direction*). Hello, Mr Downing.

RUSSELL. Bradwell.

BRADWELL. Are you having a good day?

RUSSELL. Marvellous. Thank you.

BRADWELL. That's alright, don't you worry about it.

BRADWELL finds a high stool to sit on. DENISE *has also moved across to the bar, though is still keeping a bit of distance from* BRADWELL.

JIM. Piss-weak lager then?

BRADWELL. Yes please, boss.

BRADWELL nods.

JIM starts to pour him a drink.

DENISE. So you don't know what happened?

BRADWELL. Sort of but I just woke up so I'm still a bit…

BRADWELL gestures vaguely with his hands.

DENISE. Yeah, you do look a bit…

DENISE does a delicate, mini-version of BRADWELL's *gesture.*

BRADWELL. I am, yeah.

JIM. What's the last thing you remember?

BRADWELL. Er…

BRADWELL considers.

JIM (*having poured the lager*). There you go.

BRADWELL. Thank you so much.

> BRADWELL *takes a sip. It clearly takes the edge off a bit.*
> BRADWELL *exhales and gathers himself.*

> (*Searching his brain.*) The last thing I remember. The last
> thing I, remember. The last thing. I remember. The last...
> That I... Is...

> BRADWELL *gestures vaguely and grimaces as he searches*
> *for the answer.*

> *Suddenly the movement of these gestures gets slightly clearer*
> *and more deliberate as* BRADWELL *starts to work through*
> *the memory.*

> I got it I got it I got it I got it.

DENISE. What?

BRADWELL. Yeah, I was in the pub. This pub.

JIM. Yeah.

BRADWELL. Yeah, I was in the pub, I come to the pub.

JIM. Good start, Bradders, but not a massive shock.

BRADWELL. No.

DENISE. Do ya remember anything else?

BRADWELL. Erm... No.

DENISE. But when did you come here though?

BRADWELL. Ooh. It was last night, yeah. (*It starts coming*
back to him as he says it.) Coz... coz I tried on this suit at
home just to see what it looked like but I was like, yeah, I
look like fucking good actually, like James Bond or something, so I'm gonna get me some *Octo-pussy*. Well, not really
I'm very happy with Amy and she meets all my emotional
and sexual needs 'n' that but like this is my brother's suit and
I never wore like a black suit like this yeah apart from when
I didn't pay that TV licence so yeah go to The Swan see

who's around bap bap bap bap see what they think of the garb, *bosh*. But it got quite. Yeah. Messy.

JIM. So you been here all night?

BRADWELL *considers this*.

BRADWELL. Is it the morning now?

JIM. Afternoon.

BRADWELL. Then I must have, yeah. Is it Saturday?

DENISE. *Yes*.

JIM. So why didn't Nick clear you out?

BRADWELL. He was more pissed than anyone, mate.

JIM. He's losing it.

BRADWELL. Yeah, at one point he actually brought his laptop down and was showing us all these videos. There was one with a cup.

JIM. Of what?

BRADWELL. I don't really wanna talk about it. Those poor girls.

JIM. I always think that.

BRADWELL. Yeah, and then Nick just got really really pissed and started looking sad and stuff and went upstairs cuddling his laptop but before he went he said he didn't really care any more and fuck the brewery in the eye and we could all just drink and do what we liked. He didn't even lock the door or gives us the keys or nothing so we all just got a bit cunted yeah – I ate a lot o' crisps – and then I musta gone to the toilet for some sleep, you know for a bit o' quiet time. Though then there was some noise and all this like clanging when it got light.

JIM (*referring to all the food*). That'll've been the Indian pizza boys, bringing all that in.

BRADWELL. Oh right, I thought it might be some ghosts.

JIM. Ghosts?

BRADWELL. Yeah.

JIM. Bradwell, how the fuck did you get to your age still believing in ghosts?

BRADWELL. I have a very protective mother.

JIM shakes his head/sighs/half-smiles.

The door opens and AMY *enters.*

AMY. Bradwell.

BRADWELL. Amy.

AMY. What ya doing?

BRADWELL. Drinking. Do you want one?

AMY. No I don't.

BRADWELL. We might have some crisps left, somewhere?

AMY. Do I look like I want some cheese-and-onion fucking crisps, Bradwell?

A brief pause.

BRADWELL. No. (*To* JIM/DENISE.) This is Amy.

JIM. Yeah.

AMY. So?

BRADWELL. What?

AMY. So what happened, Bradwell? You said we were going go out today: just you and me.

BRADWELL. Did I?

AMY nods.

AMY. Yeah, that's why I gone round yours just now but your mum says you ain't even been home yet. Then some girl answers your phone. *Then* I come here to find you looking like George fucking Best two days after he's fucking died.

BRADWELL. Oh right, yeah.

AMY. Don't you remember, last night, Bradwell?

BRADWELL. Erm…

AMY. You called me – woke me up – and we talked for forty-
five fucking minutes, Bradwell, at two in the fucking
morning. Make a day of it, you said. London Eye. Fucking…
Nobu, whatever that is. You were going on about it for
fucking time. (*Doing a very mock*-BRADWELL.) 'It'll be all
like fucking special romantic, babes.' All that cunt out your
mouth.

BRADWELL. Oh right. Okay. Right. Yeah yeah. The thing is,
Amy, right? I am feeling a little bit under the the old, erm…

AMY. No no no no no no no you know what, Bradwell, I've
had it. For a fucking lifetime I've had it. We've only been
going out two months!

BRADWELL *nods*.

BRADWELL. Yeah. Okay. I understand.

AMY. Do ya?

BRADWELL.…yeah.

AMY *shakes her head*.

AMY. You know what? I've gone past being fucking
disappointed in you, Bradwell. (*Gesturing over her
shoulder*.) It's there, behind me.

BRADWELL.…?

AMY. Can you see it?

BRADWELL. What?

AMY. The mountain of fucking disappointment that's built up,
like fucking. Snowdinia.

BRADWELL.…

AMY. Can ya see it?

BRADWELL *nods*.

BRADWELL....I can, yeah.

AMY. Well, I fucking can't no more, coz it's too far fucking back.

BRADWELL. Right.

AMY. Yeah. *Yes*. You...

AMY *shakes her head/sighs*.

A pause.

Who's all them then?

BRADWELL. Erm. Just some people. Nice people. Jim, Denise and Mr Downing.

JIM *and* DENISE *hold up their hands briefly (as a small wave 'hello')*.

RUSSELL. Hello.

DENISE. Hey.

AMY (*to* JIM/RUSSELL/DENISE). Yeah. (*Back to* BRADWELL.) I mean, look at the state of you.

RUSSELL *goes back to his paper*.

BRADWELL. I know.

AMY. Embarrassment.

BRADWELL. I know, yeah.

AMY. To yourself. To me. To mankind, bruv. Womankind. Childrenkind. Allthefuckingkinds.

BRADWELL. Right.

AMY. So why do you keep doing these fucking things for?

BRADWELL. It's just the way I've like... evolved.

AMY. No, Bradwell, it isn't, you're just a fuck-up, plain and simple.

BRADWELL. I know, yeah.

JIM. (Jesus Christ, Denise.)

DENISE (*to* AMY). It's nice to… to meet you.

AMY. Yeah, I said that, dint I?

   AMY *takes in the pub a little.*

   So this is your local then?

BRADWELL. It is, yeah.

AMY. Think I been here, yeah.

BRADWELL. Do you like it?

AMY. No, Bradwell.

BRADWELL. Why not?

AMY. Coz you're in it.

JIM. Oi, come on, girl, give him a fucking.

AMY. What? Give him a what?

JIM. A break.

AMY. I will, yeah. And what is that smell?

BRADWELL. Erm… It might be my…

JIM. It's the drains. They've. Backlogged. Comes wafting
   through, sometimes.

BRADWELL. Yeah.

AMY. Reeks.

   BRADWELL *mouths 'thank you' to* JIM.

JIM. They've been on to the brewery but, what can ya do?

DENISE. Yeah.

AMY. Were you the girl on the phone?

DENISE. Yeah.

AMY. Yeah. And what's all this food out for? Having a fucking
   party?

JIM. It's all question with you, innit?

AMY. Yeah it is, yeah. So who's it for then?

JIM. Us.

AMY. I got that bit. Why? (*To* DENISE.) Is it your birthday then?

DENISE. No.

AMY. Yeah yeah it is, coz you're all dressed up, like some little…

DENISE. It ain't my birthday.

AMY. Must be, look at ya.

JIM. It ain't.

AMY. All in black: so what, did someone die or something?

DENISE. Yeah.

AMY. *No*. Why didn't you fucking tell me that, Bradwell?

BRADWELL. Erm, I was gonna but…

JIM (*to* BRADWELL). Fucking hell, mate, have you got a leash for this one?

BRADWELL. No, I haven't.

AMY (*to* JIM). For your information, I've actually got attention deficit hyperactivity disorder ADHD so you cunt talking like that is actually fucking offensive to my fucking condition, okay?

JIM (*can't help but laugh*). Er… Okay then.

AMY (*to* DENISE, *suddenly softening/calming*). So who was it?

DENISE. What?

AMY. Who met death.

No response. AMY *looks around at them*.

Ain't that a fair fucking question?

DENISE. Yeah. I suppose. It was my...

AMY *gestures delicately for* DENISE *to carry on.*

AMY....?

DENISE....my sort o' step-dad.

AMY (*seemingly genuine, with her hand on her heart*). Oh dear. Oh, sadness.

JIM. Mindful of your. Condition. Would a drink help keep you calm?

AMY. Na na, alcohol sends me the other way. I get a bit.

BRADWELL. It does. She can be a right handful, sometimes.

JIM. How about an elephant gun?

AMY. Is that a cocktail?

JIM. No.

AMY (*to* JIM, *very much getting it*). Then I don't get it. (*To* DENISE, *calm as you like*.) What was his name, love?

DENISE. Who?

AMY. The guy who.

DENISE....why?

AMY. Coz I know people, dun I? All over.

DENISE....Michael.

AMY. Michael. Michael what?

JIM. Thomas.

AMY. Michael, Thomas?

JIM. Yeah.

AMY. Was he quite tall?

DENISE. Yeah.

AMY. Was he white?

JIM. Yeah.

AMY (*gesturing to her arm*). And he had like a weird Maori tattoo thing, here?

JIM. Yeah. You know him?

AMY. *Yeah*, Micky fucking T? Everyone knows him. Like, fucking. Famous.

DENISE. What for?

AMY. Is he really like fucking dead 'n' that?

JIM. Oi oi, girl, please.

AMY. What?

JIM. Amy, whatever. Satan. You seem like you've had one too many Skittles and that's that's fair enough – that's your fucking EU human rights as a... disabled, I get that – but this is a a a reception, right? Mark of respect for the boy.

AMY. So?

JIM. So you tone it down then, alright?

AMY. I am.

JIM. Downer.

AMY. What, you telling me off?

JIM. Yeah.

AMY. Are you gonna spank me on my pudendum?

JIM. No, but I'll hit you in the face.

BRADWELL. Jim.

JIM. *Well.*

AMY. Are you threatening me now?

JIM (*softening*). No no, I'm just... I'm just telling ya. Aren't I? Fair warning. Tread. Careful.

AMY. This is me treading very fucking careful.

JIM. Well then, tread very. Fucking. Carefuller. Okay?

A brief pause.

AMY. Whatever. So how did he?

AMY *does a vague gesture to represent 'death'.*

DENISE. Car crash. He'd been drinking. He was driving. On his own.

AMY *nods.*

AMY. He liked a drink.

DENISE. Yeah. How do you… know him?

AMY. Oh yeah, I used to fuck him a bit. Here and there.

BRADWELL. *Amy.*

AMY (*to* BRADWELL). Yes, Bradwell?

DENISE. When? When did you…?

AMY. Ages ago.

DENISE. When though?

AMY. Like, two year back. Why, how long's he been with your mum for?

DENISE. Twelve years.

A brief pause.

AMY. Well, this is a bit fucking awkward then, isn't it?

JIM. Yeah.

AMY. Yeah.

DENISE *nods.*

DENISE.…

BRADWELL. Did you love him, Amy?

AMY *gives* BRADWELL *a savage look.*

AMY. Tit.

DENISE. How long did you see him for?

AMY. 'Bout. Six months. On and off.

JIM. Don't... do not...

AMY. What? I'm answering her question.

JIM. Well...

AMY. I'm being fucking civil 'n' that, in I?

JIM. *Well, fucking don't then.*

AMY. *One minute you're saying I'm too loud, now you're saying I'm too fucking civil.* Jesus Christ, make up your mind!

DENISE (*to* JIM). Did you know about her?

JIM. No. Course not. Never seen her before, thank God.

AMY. *Oi.* I am here.

BRADWELL. Yeah, she is here, Jim.

JIM. Yeah.

DENISE. Did he mention. That he had a family?

AMY. Na na, he was too pissed to speak most the time. Why I knocked it on the head.

DENISE. He didn't talk about us?

JIM. Denise.

AMY. Well, he wouldn't, would he?

DENISE. No, I suppose he...

JIM. Please. Just don't... say, any more.

AMY. Depends, what she asks me though, don' it?

JIM. Yeah, okay. Denise. That's enough now. Let's leave it. Michael obviously... But let's not... Dig up... Eh?

DENISE. You said he was famous.

AMY. Yeah. Well, not like *Big Brother* telly famous but. You know.

DENISE. No. What?

JIM. Girl.

DENISE *shoots a stare at* JIM.

AMY *shrugs*.

AMY. He got about.

DENISE *nods*.

DENISE. With, women?

AMY. Yeah. Not with men, I don't think. Unless he really got about.

JIM (*to* AMY). What did I say?

AMY. What?

DENISE. Do you wanna a drink?

AMY. Bit early for me.

DENISE. It's free.

JIM. Not for her it ain't.

AMY. Is it?

DENISE *nods*.

JIM. No.

AMY. I'll have a very large vodka and cranberry then please.

JIM. No. No, you won't.

AMY. She said.

JIM *shakes his head*.

DENISE. Make her one. Or I will.

A slight stand-off before JIM *grudgingly starts to make a vodka and cranberry.*

AMY. With ice, please. And a straw.

JIM *nods*.

DENISE. When did you last see him?

AMY. About a year ago. He tried it on with me but I weren't having none of it, not really.

BRADWELL. (Fuck.)

DENISE. Did you hear anything else about him?

AMY. Yeah, he was seeing some girl out near Kent or something.

JIM *and* DENISE *share a look*.

Is that where your mum lives then?

JIM. No.

DENISE. He died driving out that way.

JIM (*to* AMY, *about the drink*). There's you go.

AMY (*taking it*). Thank you.

DENISE. Do you know her name? This girl in Kent?

AMY. No.

DENISE. Was it. Tasha?

AMY. I dunno. No idea.

JIM (*to* DENISE). How do you…?

DENISE *stares at* JIM.

BRADWELL. Who's Tasha? Was she at the funeral?

JIM. No, Bradwell.

DENISE *heads to the toilet, opens the door. Pauses briefly*.

DENISE. Bradwell, did you do anything in the girls?

BRADWELL. No.

JIM. Denise.

JIM *moves towards* DENISE.

DENISE *nods to* BRADWELL *and goes into the toilets*.

BRADWELL. I don't think so, anyway.

A pause as the dust settles.

JIM (*to* AMY). Happy then?

AMY. It's better to know these things, innit?

JIM. *No.*

AMY. Yeah. Can I get a slice o' lime in this?

JIM *shakes his head*.

JIM. No, you can go fucking swivel.

AMY. Why?

JIM. Because you just told her all that...

AMY. So what? She asked me.

JIM. I don't care.

AMY. Well, you should.

JIM. Why?

AMY. Because it's the truth.

JIM. I didn't tell her the truth because I knew it'd break her... little... fucking...

AMY. The truth always finds a way, though.

JIM. Does it?

AMY *nods*.

BRADWELL *nods*.

BRADWELL. George Goldblum says that in *Jurassic Park*.

JIM. Great. Thanks for your combined input.

RUSSELL (*about* DENISE). Is she, alright?

JIM. Yeah, she'll be... she'll be fine.

AMY. Maybe I should go in there, have a little word with her.

JIM. No, you've had enough little fucking words.

AMY. Ain't my fault, is it? It's Micky.

JIM. Yeah, but I was keeping a lid on his...

BRADWELL. On his what?

JIM.... activities.

BRADWELL. What activities?

JIM. Penetrating... half of South-East England.

BRADWELL. Oh. Right. (Jeff Goldblum, sorry.)

AMY. So you knew?

JIM. I might have had an inkling, yeah.

BRADWELL. Was he penetrating Tasha? Whoever that is.

A pointed lack of response from JIM, *during which he pours himself another drink and/or lights up a cigarette.*

AMY. Why you keeping a lid on it for anyway? Serves him right, if you ask me.

BRADWELL. Coz Michael was his son.

AMY. No wonder you're upset then. Coz he's making you look like a right fucking twat, inny?

JIM *nods. Laughs.*

JIM. I think that's the first thing you've said I've actually agreed with.

AMY *gestures to the cigarette.*

AMY. Can I pinch one?

A brief pause.

JIM. Go on.

JIM *takes out a cigarette, hands it to* AMY, *who lights up.*

BRADWELL. I thought you give up.

AMY. You drove me to it, mate. (*To* JIM.) So you allowed to smoke in this pub then? You got like a special licence or something?

BRADWELL. No.

AMY. I was asking him, Bradwell.

BRADWELL....

JIM. No.

AMY. Oh right. So you just do it?

JIM. Yeah.

AMY. Cool.

> DENISE *appears in the toilet doorway.*

AMY (*drawing attention to* DENISE). Oo' eyah.

> JIM *sees* DENISE.

JIM. You alright?

DENISE (*to* JIM). What do you know?

AMY. He knows it all, babe.

JIM. Oi.

DENISE. And what is that?

AMY. That Micky was...

DENISE. Jim.

JIM. Look. I didn't know much for... for definite.

DENISE. But you knew something?

JIM....maybe.

DENISE. I thought you might. Why you didn't tell Mum?

JIM. What could I tell her?

DENISE. All of it.

AMY. Yeah.

DENISE. And you've heard about. Tasha?

JIM. ... who is that? No.

DENISE. Be honest.

A pause.

JIM. The name might have come up, yeah.

DENISE. Was he on his way to her, when he... ?

JIM. ... yeah.

DENISE. How do you... know that?

JIM. Coz I dealt with the... all the police, side of things. She was the last person he... he called.

AMY. Well, isn't this fucking fascinating?

JIM. Look, will you smoke that outside or something?

AMY. No. This is just getting good.

JIM. I'm not asking you, alright? Please.

BRADWELL. Yeah, maybe we could go for a nice walk, babes.

AMY. Bradwell, if you even come anywhere near me, I will stab you in your face.

BRADWELL. Right.

JIM. Seriously, fuck off now, girl, okay?

AMY. Don't blame me! You the one been sneaky-beaky lying all over the fucking place. (*About* DENISE.) To that poor little lady there. And her fucking mum.

DENISE. Yeah.

JIM. *I know* but...

AMY. So why you taking it out on me then?

JIM. Look, fucking... Look. Please. This is difficult enough as it is... without...

AMY. Well, whose fault's that?

A brief pause.

JIM. Okay. It's fucking... not yours, really. But you're not exactly fucking helping, are ya?

AMY. I reckon I am though, yeah.

JIM. That wasn't up for debate, alright?

AMY. So?

A brief pause.

JIM. Bradwell?

BRADWELL. What?

JIM. Please.

BRADWELL. What?

JIM sighs.

A brief pause.

JIM. Denise, can you help me out here, then?

DENISE. No.

A brief pause.

AMY. On your own.

JIM. Yeah.

AMY. I told ya: the truth comes out.

JIM. That's it: I warned ya.

As he says this, JIM *either advances on* AMY, *or stands (if he's been sitting). The mood turns.*

Get. Fucking. Out. Okay?

BRADWELL. Jim.

AMY. Here we go then.

JIM. Yeah. Go.

AMY. Typical.

JIM. What is?

AMY. See old cunts like you all the time. In my pub. Throwing their weight around.

JIM. Well, that's what I'm doing.

AMY. Yeah. Coz Micky was like that. Kicked off enough times. Over nothing.

JIM. This ain't nothing. S'important.

AMY. Yeah, he'd say that, too.

A pause.

JIM. ...I'm begging you.

AMY. No need. Didn't wanna hang round here anyway, did I?

JIM. (Expect not.)

AMY. Shithole.

AMY *finishes her drink. Starts to go.*

And you know what I like about people like you?

JIM. What's that?

AMY. Nothing. And I ain't the only one, oh, I can tell that. Yeah, I can see right through ya. Coz you're just like him – Micky – all fucking mouth, no fucking heart. You know?

JIM *nods slightly.*

AMY *nods.*

Yeah. So you ain't fucking worth it, are ya?

JIM. No.

AMY (*a brief pause. To* DENISE). Are you gonna be alright alone with all these stupid fucking cunts, sweetie?

DENISE *nods.*

DENISE. Thank you.

AMY. What for?

DENISE. For being honest.

AMY. Pleasure. Well, you were.

AMY *starts to back out of the pub*. BRADWELL *starts to moves towards her.*

BRADWELL. Petal.

AMY. Don't make me hurt you, Bradwell, okay?

BRADWELL *nods.*

BRADWELL. Yeah. Okay, Amy. Yeah.

AMY *nods.*

AMY. Good. (*Shakes her head.*) Nobu.

AMY *goes.*

JIM *shakes his head.*

BRADWELL *downs the remains of his drink. Starts to head after* AMY.

JIM. Where you going?

BRADWELL. After her.

JIM. She just threatened ya life, mate, pretty much.

BRADWELL. Yeah, but she's always doing that. And you weren't very nice to her, so… And anyway, she's all I've got. Apart from my family. And my friends. And everyone at work.

RUSSELL. You'll pull through somehow, Bradwell.

BRADWELL. Do ya think?

RUSSELL. I'd bet my wife's life on it.

BRADWELL. Oh. Thank you, Mr Downing.

RUSSELL. 'S alright.

BRADWELL. Bye then.

BRADWELL *goes.*

JIM. Bye, Bradwell, you stupid fucking. Mong.

JIM *shakes his head.*

DENISE. He isn't.

JIM. What just happened, Mr Downing? Seriously. I was having a quiet fucking drink.

RUSSELL. Events.

JIM. Yeah, when will they ever fucking. Stop.

A pause.

DENISE. Did she live in Sevenoaks?

JIM. Erm. Yeah. How do you...?

DENISE. I used to hear him on the phone to her, sometimes. When Mum was out.

JIM. Christ.

DENISE. Last few months, they were arguing a lot. Shouting. I think she wanted money from him or something.

JIM. Right.

DENISE. Why would he owe her money?

JIM. You knew Michael. Could be... could be anything. I don't know.

A pause.

DENISE. We have to tell her.

JIM. Who?

DENISE. Mum.

JIM. You taking the piss?

DENISE. No.

JIM. The day she's had and you wanna...?

DENISE. Yeah.

JIM. Why?

DENISE. Because.

JIM. So what, you wanna tell her Michael was fucking his way through the phone book?

DENISE *nods*.

DENISE. She should... she should know.

JIM. No, she shouldn't. Least not today, of all fucking...

DENISE. I nearly did.

JIM. What?

DENISE. This morning.

JIM. What were you gonna...?

DENISE. About her.

JIM. Yeah, okay. And why didn't ya?

DENISE. I don't...

JIM. Yeah, you do.

DENISE....because I didn't know exactly what I knew.

JIM. Yeah, you did. You're fucking smart. You knew what Michael was like and... you obviously knew what he was fucking up to. The reason you didn't tell your mum this morning is because that would be the act of a cunt.

RUSSELL. Mr Thomas.

JIM. Wouldn't it?

DENISE....

JIM. Fucking. Cruel, to her.

DENISE. But what if she heard today though, from someone else?

JIM. She won't.

DENISE. You know that?

JIM. Yeah.

DENISE. How?

JIM. Because I'll watch out for her.

DENISE. Like you did this morning?

JIM. No – no – that ain't the same.

DENISE. Why not?

JIM. That was just coz I don't like... I don't like... funerals. 'N' that.

DENISE. You're still saying, that's why you didn't go?

JIM....

Pause.

No. Obviously not. Look, Mr Downing can hear every fucking word we're...

DENISE. I don't care.

JIM. Well, I do.

RUSSELL. You know I won't tell a soul.

JIM. Yeah, but...

JIM*'s Nokia phone starts to go.*

Oh, Christ up a... Mexican...

JIM *takes the phone out.*

DENISE. Who is it?

JIM. Your mum.

DENISE *moves towards* JIM/*the phone.*

(*To* DENISE, *stopping her.*) Not a word.

JIM *starts to move towards the double doors, putting a bit of distance between him and* DENISE.

God fucking help me. Or the Devil. Someone. Anyone. *Anneka?*

JIM *looks at* DENISE *once last time before answering it and heading towards the exit/entrance.*

Hello, love. You alright? (*Listens.*) Of course.

JIM *exits, though we get glimpses of him just outside the double doors.*

A pause before DENISE *and* RUSSELL *are suddenly aware of each other.* RUSSELL *looks up from his crossword. Smiles.*

DENISE *goes behind the bar to make herself another vodka and Coke. As she does, she initiates the following:*

DENISE. Do you want a top-up?

RUSSELL. I'm alright but, thank you.

DENISE (*referring to his crossword*). How can you do that with everyone like around you?

RUSSELL. Just background noise, really. Quite like it. Reminds me of the nineties.

DENISE. What happened then?

RUSSELL. The boys were still at home.

DENISE. You have kids?

RUSSELL *nods.*

RUSSELL. Two.

DENISE. Are they old?

RUSSELL. They're both doing PhDs up in The North.

DENISE. Wow.

RUSSELL. Adam and Daniel, yeah.

DENISE. Are you proud of them?

RUSSELL. Of Daniel, yes.

DENISE. But not...?

RUSSELL *shakes his head.*

RUSSELL. Adam has a permanent sort of sneer.

DENISE. Right.

RUSSELL. Which he didn't get from me.

DENISE. Right. (*A brief pause.*) I don't know your name, not really. They only ever call you Mr Downing.

RUSSELL. Oh yeah, er: Russell.

DENISE. Denise.

RUSSELL. I know. (*Pause.*) Do you miss him?

DENISE. Jim?

RUSSELL. Michael.

DENISE *shrugs.*

DENISE. ...complicated, what I feel. I know he loved us, but. He was so...

RUSSELL *nods.*

RUSSELL. British disease that.

DENISE. What?

RUSSELL. We understand the complexity of things and act accordingly. On the continent they cry and wail all the time about nothing because they don't know what's going on, not really. Italians. French. Spanish. Greeks. Overemotional children, really. The Germans and Scandinavians can be better, but often they're even worse.

DENISE. So we're the best?

RUSSELL. Absolutely.

DENISE *smiles a little.*

'To wear your heart on your sleeve isn't a very good plan; you should wear it inside, where it functions best.'

DENISE. Is that like a Buddhist thing?

RUSSELL. Not quite. Margaret Thatcher. 1987.

DENISE *smiles fades*.

DENISE. Oh.

RUSSELL. She wasn't all bad, you know?

DENISE. No?

RUSSELL. No. No one is, not really.

DENISE *shrugs a little*.

DENISE. I wasn't even born.

RUSSELL *nods*.

A brief pause.

RUSSELL. Don't worry though, Denise. You are loved.

DENISE. What?

RUSSELL. I hear enough to know. Loved deeply. If not always
wisely.

DENISE. Okay.

RUSSELL. Which is rare. Precious.

DENISE. Okay.

DENISE *has by now made her drink. She spots the iPhone*.

(*As she picks it up*.) Bradwell left his phone. I should go after
him.

RUSSELL. No, it's alright: that's Jim's.

DENISE *shakes her head*.

DENISE. It isn't.

RUSSELL. Yeah, he was playing with it I came in.

DENISE. But he's on his phone now.

RUSSELL. I saw he had two, I just thought he was in a.
Transition stage.

DENISE *is going through the phone.*

A pause.

What's wrong?

A brief pause.

DENISE. I think it's Michael's.

A long-ish pause.

DENISE *is going through the texts, finds a picture (the same that* JIM *was looking at earlier).*

RUSSELL. Are you okay?

JIM *appears back in the doorway, as he puts his Nokia phone away.*

It has started to rain outside and JIM *is a tiny amount wet.*

JIM. Do you smoke, Mr Downing?

RUSSELL. No, I have respiratory problems.

JIM. Right, well, can you pretend to smoke?

RUSSELL. Erm. Yeah. I don't see why not.

JIM *offers* RUSSELL *a cigarette.*

JIM (*referring to the doorway*). Simple job then: stand out there, and if you see Christine coming, you let me know, okay?

RUSSELL (*standing and taking the cigarette*). Oh. Alright, yeah.

JIM. You do know what she looks like?

RUSSELL. Yeah. Yes.

JIM. Thank you then. Go on. I'll make it up to ya. (One day.)

RUSSELL *moves towards the doorway, though hovers slightly on the inside of it (rather than stepping completely outside) and at some point maybe even returns briefly to get his coat (or something from it).*

JIM *moves towards* DENISE.

DENISE. What you doing?

JIM. She's on her way. Yeah. And she wants to rip my cock and balls off just using her thumbs. So I think she's got enough on her plate to be getting on with. You know? (*A brief pause.*) Come on, talk to me, girl. We got about five minutes before she gets here. She knows you're here. We can't tell her. We can't. Let's just agree that now and sort it all out tomorrow. Okay? (*Pause.*) Okay?

DENISE *shakes her head.*

Why not?

DENISE *holds up the iPhone, shows* JIM *the image of a one-year-old child.*

DENISE. Who's that?

JIM....? ...Where'd you get that?

DENISE. You told Mum the police lost it. (*Pause.*) Who is he?

JIM. Look, she'll be here, any second.

DENISE. Who? Is it?

JIM....(*Pause.*) Jake.

DENISE. And who's that?

A pause.

JIM. Michael and Tasha's. Kid.

RUSSELL. Oh dear.

JIM. Yeah. (*Realising that* RUSSELL *isn't properly in position.*) Look, smoke it outside and keep fucking watch!

RUSSELL *nods and hurriedly retreats outside with his unlit cigarette (though from hereon in – as he fake-smokes outside – he occasionally looks in to check on* JIM *and* DENISE).

A brief pause.

DENISE. How long have you known?

A long pause.

JIM. A year.

DENISE. Is that why she wanted money?

JIM *nods.*

Have you met him?

JIM....

JIM *nods.*

Once, yeah.

DENISE. How?

JIM. I gave him – Michael – a lift to the hospital, when Jake was fucking like. Born.

DENISE. But you didn't see him again?

JIM. No.

DENISE. Why?

JIM. Tasha didn't really take to me.

DENISE. Why not?

JIM. Coz I tried to warn her. About Michael.

DENISE. You did?

JIM. Yeah.

DENISE. What, because she deserved the truth?

JIM. Dee. It's different.

DENISE. Is it?

JIM. Course it is.

DENISE. No, it isn't.

JIM. I wanted to. I did. You and your mum. But...

DENISE. But what?

JIM....I dunno.

DENISE. Is that all you got?

JIM *shrugs*.

JIM....

DENISE. You can talk for England and now you can't even...

JIM. How do ya bring something like that up?

DENISE. How do you not?

JIM. No no, look. You knew something. You heard those calls. You didn't tell her.

DENISE. That isn't the same... thing. I didn't meet the...

JIM. Course it is. You wanted to protect her. Not cause her any unnecessary, like...

DENISE. Unnecessary?

JIM. Dee.

DENISE. Wait till she finds out. She will actually kill you.

JIM. She doesn't need to though, does she? Not now. Not yet.

DENISE. Yes, she does.

JIM. Look – Denise – I don't want a row.

DENISE. Well, you've fucking got one.

JIM. Just let her have today, okay?

DENISE. You mean, let you have today?

JIM. No. No.

DENISE. And let her have being a fool again?

JIM. She's not being a fucking fool, is she?

DENISE. I know, but you're making her one.

JIM. I'm not, I'm fucking... I'm protecting her. No one will say anything to her. Not today. I promise you.

DENISE. That's not... that's not good enough.

JIM. Well, it'll... it'll have to be.

DENISE. You know... (*A brief pause.*) I thought you didn't go today because you didn't wanna hear all those people saying all those lies 'bout him, eulogies and... When you knew what he could be like, to us. Like the way he'd talk about me when I was there, like I was some... So I left Mum – alone with all them people – coz I thought – in some way – that was somehow. Like. Brave, of you, or... And I didn't wanna hear all that, either, you know? Let alone. Say it.

JIM. Dee.

DENISE. Did I?

JIM. No.

DENISE. After twelve years of... But it turns out he was even worse than I... Than I... Ever... And you could have told us that.

JIM. I couldn't...

DENISE. But you decided just to... to let us... To let him off. You helped him, do that to us.

JIM. *No.*

DENISE. You did.

JIM. Denise.

DENISE. I hate you, so much.

JIM. I know you do, but... Please.

A pause.

DENISE. Why didn't you stop him?

JIM. Michael?

DENISE. Yeah.

JIM. Stop what?

DENISE. All of it.

JIM. You seriously think that... that if I could have said something to him – done something – to make him change his... I wouldn't have? Few words. Few words in his fucking... That I wouldn't... That I wouldn't fucking bother, or...? Is that what you think?

RUSSELL *tentatively comes back into the doorway.*

RUSSELL. Are you two... happy, in here?

JIM. Yes, mate, now fuck off and do your job, I told ya.

RUSSELL....Denise?

DENISE *nods.*

RUSSELL *nods and tentatively goes back outside.*

JIM (*back to* DENISE). So?

DENISE. You never even tried to stop him.

JIM. I didn't?

DENISE. No.

JIM. And why not?

DENISE. Coz you were...

JIM. What?

A brief pause.

DENISE....scared of him.

JIM....was I?

DENISE. Yeah. Like I was. Yeah.

JIM. You were scared of him?

DENISE. Of course I was. I hated him.

JIM. Hang on. He didn't like hurt you, or...?

DENISE. No. But he would lose it all the time, about anything. Make the whole flat, like... so... Just by being there. And I never knew what to say, what would make him like start off again, or... Tried to sleep, whenever it was – even in the day – but he was so... And Mum would just blame herself, for whatever made him upset. Even if *he'd* done something, he would turn it against her. I'd hear him. Through the walls. You know?

JIM. Yeah. That's why Jackie – his mum – she left, in the... in the fucking end. She couldn't stand it, when he... got like that.

DENISE. I know. And it's why you were scared of him, too.

JIM. ...maybe.

DENISE. Yes. It was.

JIM. Okay. But so what, eh? Now. He's gone. Isn't he? We can...

DENISE. 'So what?'

JIM. No, I didn't mean it like that, I'm not...

DENISE. You did though. You do.

JIM. No.

DENISE. You know what?

JIM. What?

DENISE. Amy was right.

JIM. (What about, *Jurassic Park*?)

DENISE. No. You and Michael. (*A brief pause.*) You're just like him.

JIM. No. We were chalk and fucking...

DENISE. Yeah. You are.

A pause.

JIM. Why?

DENISE. Coz you'll do anything, say anything. To hide from what you done.

JIM. No.

DENISE. That's all you do. Like today, leaving Mum to deal with your family and then trying to turn it all into some joke. 'Oh, I don't do funerals.'

RUSSELL *has come back into the room.*

JIM (*to* RUSSELL). Is she coming?

RUSSELL. No, I was just still concerned about you and...

JIM. Get to fuck then!

RUSSELL *nods.*

RUSSELL. I will, I'll, erm... get. Yeah.

RUSSELL *goes back outside.*

A pause.

DENISE. And not telling us about Jake. When that could have... saved us. From him.

JIM. No, no, the reason I didn't... The reason that I...

DENISE. What? Why not?

JIM. Because... (*Pause.*) Because if I'd told ya, you would – you and your mum – would have... You would have... left me. Wouldn't ya? Like they all fucking do.

DENISE. Yeah.

JIM. And I'd'a been alone again with. Michael. And Bradwell. And fucking. Nick.

DENISE. Yeah.

JIM. So that's why... why I didn't. You know?

DENISE. That isn't good enough.

JIM. I think it is, though.

DENISE *shakes her head.*

DENISE. But isn't even just that. Like. You never say *anything* important. You've never told me you love me. (*Pause.*) You act like I'm just your mate, or something. You never asked me what happened at school. What they did to me.

JIM. I didn't want you to… to rake over it, love.

DENISE. No, you just pretended it was like, bit o' fun. Some scrapes.

JIM. You're alright though.

DENISE. No, I'm not.

JIM. Look at ya.

DENISE. Yeah.

JIM. Tough little… You're tough, intya? Like your mum. Like me.

DENISE. No.

JIM. You are, girl.

DENISE. No, I got… broken. That school. I started to tell you once but you just pretended like you couldn't hear me.

A pause.

JIM. Look. Everyone be here soon. Your mum. All the guests. Let's not…

DENISE. I don't care.

JIM. Well, I do.

DENISE. Coz you're all I've got. My real dad, God knows where he is. Michael is literally in the ground now. So you're all I have. And look at you.

JIM. Dee.

DENISE. So why bother?

JIM. What?

DENISE. Why hang around?

JIM. What you talking about?

DENISE. Why stay here?

JIM. Translate.

DENISE. Why not go to the bookies, or go home? Sky Sports.

JIM. Because… Because you know why.

DENISE *shakes her head.*

DENISE. No, I don't.

A brief pause.

JIM. This is my local.

DENISE. For now.

JIM. Yeah.

DENISE. So that's your reason?

JIM. It was my mum's local. She'd bring me in here when I was little, raised me in here.

DENISE. No.

JIM. What? Course she did.

DENISE. No. Your cousins told me.

JIM. What? When?

DENISE. At Michael's thirty-first.

JIM. What did they say now?

DENISE. That Grace would drop you off in here, so she could go off on her own, somewhere. Get pissed. Find men. Come back and pick you up when she was done.

JIM. Oi.

DENISE. Everyone was saying it. Behind your back. They all say it. They do. That she only started coming back in here when she'd given up and she was drinking herself, to death. You watched it happen but you couldn't see it.

JIM. Denise, you are… you're out of order, love. You are. You can't say that, even if they… even if they fucking did.

DENISE. I am. I'm saying it. And I'm saying I think you should go. Now. I mean it.

JIM. Fuck off.

DENISE. I do.

JIM. You're being quite fucking… hurtful, Denise.

DENISE. I know.

JIM. Spiteful.

DENISE. I know, yeah.

A pause, during which JIM *lights up a cigarette.*

JIM. Who's gonna man the bar then?

DENISE. Me.

JIM. You're barely legal to drink, let alone fucking…

DENISE. You've got a criminal record.

JIM. I grazed him. It was never GBH, he could still see out of it.

DENISE. The judge thought so.

JIM *sighs.*

JIM. Yeah. But I ain't going.

DENISE. Then I will.

JIM. What?

DENISE *nods, finishes her drink and goes, passing* RUSSELL *as she does.*

(*To himself.*) Fucking hell.

A long pause.

RUSSELL *comes back in to the doorway.*

RUSSELL. Do I still need to, erm…?

JIM. No, mate. You can get on with your fucking, crossword.

RUSSELL *gives the cigarette back.*

Thank you.

RUSSELL (*referring to the crossword*). Hadn't got much done, anyway.

A pause.

JIM. I mean, is it sponsored-crazy-fucking-mental-blob-lady day, or fucking what?

RUSSELL. Not that I'm aware of.

JIM. Bet you wish you'd stayed at home.

RUSSELL. Not really, my wife and her brother are baking.

RUSSELL *shakes his head.*

JIM. What they baking?

RUSSELL. Contempt, mainly.

JIM. Tasty.

JIM *sighs.*

You want another drink? Coz I fucking do.

RUSSELL. I wouldn't mind, actually.

JIM. Another John Smith's?

RUSSELL. What else?

JIM *nods.* JIM *takes* RUSSELL*'s glass. Starts towards the bar.*

She'll get a bit soggy out there, won't she?

JIM *nods as he positions himself behind the bar. Starts to pour* RUSSELL *another.*

Poor thing.

JIM. She'll be alright. Yeah.

An extended moment, as JIM *pours.*

But then CHRISTINE *appears at the double doors, with her shoes in her hand. She is quite breathless. She catches her breath. As she does so, she ushers in* DENISE, *who she's obviously collared outside.*

CHRISTINE *has been caught up a bit in the rain, which has started to pick up a little. She looks down at her feet, which are quite dirty.* RUSSELL (*who by this point has already settled back on his table in the corner*) *catches this and hands her a handkerchief and/or lays down some newspaper to clean/wipe her feet with.*

CHRISTINE *nods and finishes putting them on. Composes herself.*

CHRISTINE. You two.

JIM. Yeah.

DENISE. Yeah.

JIM. Christine.

CHRISTINE. Don't say my name.

JIM....

JIM nods.

CHRISTINE (*to* RUSSELL). Thank you.

RUSSELL *nods.*

CHRISTINE *then starts to put her shoes on.*

RUSSELL. Very nice shoes.

CHRISTINE. Jim. That was quite a morning. Even for you.

JIM.... yeah.

CHRISTINE *shakes her head.*

CHRISTINE. I have just run. From a church. Like Linford. From *a fucking church, Jim.* You know?

JIM. Yeah.

DENISE. Yeah.

CHRISTINE. And you know what?

JIM. What's that?

A pause. CHRISTINE *is still a little breathless.*

CHRISTINE. I was… I was at my limit. At my very… I woke up this morning, and I was…

CHRISTINE *nods.*

JIM *nods.*

DENISE *nods.*

I knew today would be hard but… Even knowing that, waking up this morning. Like I'd been… I… I went to bed okay but I woke up and it hit me. Hard. (*Gesturing to her stomach.*) Here. Like I'd been shot. I couldn't… I couldn't actually stand up. I couldn't, without…

JIM. Yeah, I was like that morning o' my wedding.

CHRISTINE. No you weren't.

JIM. No, but like that. A feeling like that.

CHRISTINE. No, Jim. This is mine.

JIM. Yeah.

CHRISTINE. So it took me like half an hour to even get up. To sit up in bed. Coz the idea of… of today. I was at my limit, already. I knew that.

JIM. Right.

CHRISTINE. But I thought: 'As long as Jim keeps his cuntery to a… As long as he's even slightly quiet for me today.' Then: 'And long as Denise is okay. Then I can do this. I can do this. I'm at my limit but that's what… that's what people do. Despite all the… They do it. All around us they do it. Every day.' Don't they? (*Pause.*) Am I making sense to you?

JIM *nods.*

JIM. Yeah.

DENISE *nods*.

CHRISTINE. Good. I am glad about that because I am so… I could be speaking fucking Klingon and I wouldn't know it.

JIM. ('Make it so.')

CHRISTINE. No, Jim.

JIM. No?

CHRISTINE *shakes her head*.

CHRISTINE. No. (*A brief pause*.) So, shower, getting dressed, that was okay. Better, anyway. Getting Denise up, that was okay. She's a good girl but she could sleep for England. Olympics. Then breakfast. I couldn't eat any but Denise did, so I was…

CHRISTINE *nods*.

And I was starting to think: 'I'm at my limit but… you know, this is… this is… I can do this. I can. I can swallow this.' (*A brief pause*.) But then, then you weren't answering your phone. By the second time I called you I knew: 'He ain't… he ain't coming.' Coz you'd been giving me like little fucking clues all week. Those evasive little bullshit text messages you send. The way you'd been talking. I knew it – deep down – but. (*A brief pause*.) So now, I have to face what remains of your fucking family, on my own.

JIM. They're alright. Some of them.

CHRISTINE. I don't think a single one of them has got a full set of teeth, Jim. I'm not even joking.

JIM. (We don't like dentists.)

CHRISTINE. *Well, I don't like them.*

JIM. No.

CHRISTINE. Your cousins look like actual sex offenders.

JIM *nods*.

JIM. Yeah. They do.

CHRISTINE. And the shit, I have to eat about where you are. And I am trying to keep smiling. I am trying so hard. Little smiles. And I'm doing that for someone who's left me all on my... Making fucking excuses for you, Jim. Playing that game of... niceness. So I thought I was at my limit but turns out I had a little more in me. I've got. A bit more... There is more in me. You know? So I'm thinking: 'I'm gonna suck out Jim's eyes with one breath when I see him, but this is okay, this is just typical-him bullshit, it don't make me look bad. It's okay. I look a little bit stupid, trying to cover for him but not... I can manage this. I am managing this okay.'

JIM. You done really well. I reckon.

CHRISTINE. I did, yeah. (*A brief pause.*) So then we're sat in the pews and it starts. A lady is giving the service. Nice lady. She was good. But I'm glad I'm sat down because I'm starting to double over again. My stomach is... Again. Turning like, and... Like with a shotgun, Jim. It feels like a physical... like a fucking hole in me. And I feel like I maybe I might just... I might just... fall apart. My body might just fucking crumble into little... So I don't know what's keeping me together, Jim. Faith. Hope. Whatever. Anger. Maybe it was fucking anger. At you.

CHRISTINE *nods.*

JIM *nods.*

And then Denise goes. Says she needs the toilet. 'Desperate.' Okay. So I let her. And you know what happened? Do you know what happened?

JIM. I could have a guess.

CHRISTINE. Yeah, you could.

JIM. She... she left.

CHRISTINE. Yes. She stayed. Gone. From me. Do you know what that feels like?

JIM....

CHRISTINE. Do you?

The rain is starting to pick up even more.

JIM. I can imagine.

CHRISTINE. No. I don't think you can.

JIM....no.

CHRISTINE. I do not think you physically can.

CHRISTINE *shakes her head.*

JIM. Difficult.

CHRISTINE. There are words.

JIM. Yeah.

CHRISTINE. There are words that I could use. But difficult doesn't even begin to... You know?

JIM. Yeah.

JIM *nods.*

A pause.

You want a. A drink?

A pause.

CHRISTINE. Alright.

JIM. Gin?

CHRISTINE *nods.*

Large?

CHRISTINE *nods.*

JIM *starts to make the drink.*

CHRISTINE. With tonic.

JIM. Obviously. Sorry you had to go through... all that.

CHRISTINE. Sorry is another word.

JIM. Yeah.

CHRISTINE. And I'm done with them from you.

JIM. Yeah.

CHRISTINE (*to* DENISE). And even you, girl.

DENISE....

JIM *hands her the drink.*

CHRISTINE. Thank you.

A pause as CHRISTINE *sips her drink.*

Where was I?

DENISE. In church. On your own.

CHRISTINE. Yeah. So then I have to sit there, another however fucking long and I'm nowhere. I don't know where I am. All I know is that you'll be here: talking merry shit to fucked-up pricks. Then I call you and you've taken her.

JIM....yeah, well, she found me, yeah.

CHRISTINE. I know. Because I ran from a church, Jim. I ran in front of... funeral-goers. My parents. Other people I know and care about. That lady priest. In front of them. I ran. And when I got near here, I saw my daughter, storming away, like she's been hurt.

JIM. Yeah.

CHRISTINE. So my limit is... I don't know where it is now. And the worse thing. The very worst thing. Is that, at the church – at home – she wasn't upset. Looking like this. She wasn't. I was there. I got her through it. She was quiet. Good. I kept talking to her. I do that. I help her. But she comes here and you reduce her to that in no time. Why? What is...? What is wrong, with you?

JIM. A lot o' things.

CHRISTINE. Yeah. (*A brief pause*.) So this – now – is when you tell me what you did to her, this time. Some crack about her school, or…

JIM. We just had a little fucking… like…

CHRISTINE.…?

JIM.…tiff.

CHRISTINE. Tiff?

JIM. A little tiff, yeah.

DENISE. It wasn't.

CHRISTINE. Don't say anything. I wanna hear it from him. A little fucking tiff?

JIM. That's what I said.

CHRISTINE. You are like the perfect fucking machine, sent from the future to piss me off in every possible fucking way, you know that? *A tiff?*

JIM. Yeah.

CHRISTINE. It doesn't look like a little fucking tiff, Jim.

JIM. Well, it was.

CHRISTINE. No no. Because, for your information, my daughter doesn't tiff, Jim. She gets tiffed. By people like you.

JIM. Chris.

CHRISTINE. No no no, don't plead, don't play the… the… 'Chris.' Don't.

JIM. Chrissy.

CHRISTINE. Not today. 'Chrissy.' You cannot. I am not allowing it.

JIM. We just had a row, alright?

CHRISTINE. No, she doesn't... She is so delicate, Jim –
especially now – she doesn't... She can't cope with... Can
she?

A pause.

JIM. Rain.

CHRISTINE. What?

JIM. It's picking up.

JIM, DENISE *and* RUSSELL *look towards the double
doors, watching the rain outside* (*which has continued to get
heavier*).

CHRISTINE *has stayed focused on* JIM.

CHRISTINE. Are you even fucking listening to me?

JIM. Yeah.

CHRISTINE. So?

JIM. We were just...

CHRISTINE. Delicate, Jim. Do you even know what that
means?

JIM. Yes.

CHRISTINE. So why do you do it?

JIM. I didn't. I don't.

CHRISTINE. I saw her. I see her. What did you do?

JIM. Literally... nothing.

CHRISTINE. I don't believe you. And I am the person, you
have to make believe. You know that.

CHRISTINE *nods.*

JIM. Look, I... Yeah, you're right. I said something stupid
about her school, I was all... flippant about it. And it sort
of... 'scalated. That's true, ain't it, Denise?

A pause.

CHRISTINE. Well?

DENISE. No. It isn't.

JIM. Yeah, it is. Tell her.

DENISE. No.

A brief pause.

CHRISTINE. What is this?

A pause.

DENISE. There's something you don't know.

RUSSELL. There's something on your, on your sleeve.

CHRISTINE. Do you mind?

RUSSELL. Sorry, just a bit of fluff. Something. Bothered me.

CHRISTINE. What don't I know?

DENISE. About Michael.

CHRISTINE. What about him?

A pause.

DENISE. He had a… a… He was…

JIM. I gave him the keys.

CHRISTINE. What?

DENISE. What?

JIM. To his fucking, like. Sierra. The night he…

CHRISTINE. What are you saying?

JIM. You know he'd give me his keys when he'd had too much?

CHRISTINE. Yeah.

JIM. Well, he was in here. The night when he… And he said he
    had some… dodgy business deal, out in Kent. That he'd
    decided he couldn't go to. But then he changed his mind,
    later. Wanted 'em back. I said, 'No. Fuck off.' He tried to

scare me up a bit, but. (*A brief pause.*) Only, later on, *I* was too far gone, to. Hammered. And I left 'em lying somewhere, on me table. You know what I'm like, always leaving shit about in here. Phones, and. So I went to the toilet, come back and he'd… Yeah. He'd gone. Vanished.

CHRISTINE. Is that true?

JIM. Would I lie to you, about something like that? (*A brief pause.*) And that's why she's upset. For me. And for Michael.

CHRISTINE *looks to* DENISE.

CHRISTINE. You put that on her?

JIM. I told Denise all that, just now, yeah. I shouldn't have. I know. But I did.

CHRISTINE. So she loses a man, who's there for her, every day. She has to hold it together. She holds it together. And then you…?

JIM. Yeah. Just needed to get it off my fucking… Needed to tell someone, you know.

DENISE. Jim.

BRADWELL *arrives. He's really quite wet, from being in the rain too long.*

CHRISTINE. Bradley.

BRADWELL. Chris.

BRADWELL *heads towards the toilets.*

JIM. You alright, mate?

BRADWELL *pauses in front of the toilets.*

BRADWELL. She threw a brick at me.

JIM. It didn't get ya, though, did it?

BRADWELL. No, I'm okay. Though I am a bit wet. And I'm dying for a wee.

JIM. Yeah.

BRADWELL. Did you find my shoe yet?

JIM. No, mate.

BRADWELL. Okay then.

BRADWELL rather solemnly goes into the toilets.

CHRISTINE (*to* JIM). I don't know what to say to you.

JIM. I know.

CHRISTINE. She didn't need to be told all that, did she?

JIM shakes his head and flicks a look at DENISE.

So why would you put her through it?

JIM. I'm an idiot. You know that.

CHRISTINE. Yeah. You let Michael drive?

JIM. Yeah. And I gotta live with that. I know. He was a good man. He loved you both.

CHRISTINE. Yeah, I know.

JIM. Both of ya. Just as much as you two. Loved him. Ain't that right, Denise?

A long pause.

DENISE.…yeah. It is.

A pause, during which the rain starts to get heavier, reminiscent of the beginning of the play.

They are all now – JIM, CHRISTINE, RUSSELL, DENISE *– looking up at the roof and listening to the water hit it with a pounding, violent force. As they do,* BRADWELL *emerges from the toilet, and joins them in looking up. He has a sodden shoe in his hands.*

This looking up at the rain goes on for quite a long time. The five of them almost take on the qualities of statues. Speech is impossible/pointless and the sound/scale of the rain is fiercely impressive to listen to.

Eventually, the sound starts to fade a little and conversation is possible again.

RUSSELL. Sounds like rain.

JIM. Yeah. Found ya shoe then, mate?

BRADWELL *nods.*

BRADWELL. I think I tried to wash the sick off, in the cistern last night, but just dropped it in, then feel asleep.

JIM. Right.

DENISE. Bradwell.

BRADWELL. Yeah. Are you alright, Chris? You look a bit.

A brief pause.

CHRISTINE. Yeah, yeah. I'm... yeah. Just a tough day, you know?

BRADWELL. Yeah, obviously. I'm not interrupting anything, am I?

CHRISTINE. No.

DENISE. No.

JIM. No, mate.

BRADWELL. Good. And just so you know, I saw a load of people coming down the way. In black suits 'n' that. With brollies 'n' things. Think they might be all the guests.

CHRISTINE. They're coming?

BRADWELL. Yeah.

CHRISTINE. Look at this place. My days. We gotta tidy up. Respectable. This place. (*To* JIM.) I told you we shouldn't have it here.

JIM. I know. Sorry. Just we had my mum's wake here 'n' that, so... And it's cheap. (*A brief pause.*) Do you want a towel or something, Bradwell?

BRADWELL. I wouldn't mind.

JIM. Alright, I'll brave the elements, sure Nick's got one somewhere. (*To* CHRISTINE *and* DENISE.) You two gonna survive without me, for the moment?

CHRISTINE. Course we will.

JIM. Denise?

DENISE *looks at* JIM.

DENISE *nods.*

DENISE. Yeah.

JIM. Good girl.

(*Talking about upstairs.*) If I can brave it.

JIM *goes into the little space behind the bar. He pauses a moment.*

Ready or not, Nick! (*To himself.*) Hold your breath. And your soul.

BRADWELL. Thanks, Jim. Appreciated.

JIM. No problemo.

JIM *disappears upstairs.*

CHRISTINE. Are you okay?

DENISE *nods.*

CHRISTINE *moves towards her.* DENISE *reacts and moves away.*

DENISE. I am. I'm okay.

CHRISTINE. Ignore him, you know?

DENISE. Yeah.

DENISE *nods.*

CHRISTINE. Just a silly old man.

DENISE. No, he's just. Lonely. Scared.

CHRISTINE. That ain't an excuse.

DENISE. No. But it's why.

A brief pause.

CHRISTINE. And you do know, if there's anything I can do for you – ever – I will do it. You know that?

DENISE *nods.*

I would die for you. Don't ever doubt that about me.

DENISE. I won't. I don't.

CHRISTINE. Then we're okay.

DENISE *nods.*

A pause.

BRADWELL. Sure you two don't want a bit of quiet time, because I could go back in there for a bit, if?

CHRISTINE. No, Bradley, we're alright. We're just gonna clean up. Aren't we?

DENISE. Yeah. Course.

CHRISTINE *and* DENISE *start to clean the pub (collecting glasses, crisps packets, etc.).*

BRADWELL. I'll help.

CHRISTINE. Thank you.

BRADWELL *starts to clean up too.*

BRADWELL. And sorry for not making it, Chris. Today. You know what I'm like with. Stuff.

CHRISTINE. I do.

BRADWELL. And I'm sorry as well that I missed your reading, Denise. I bet you were dead good 'n' that.

DENISE. No, I didn't get a chance to read it, in the end.

BRADWELL. Fuck. Why not?

DENISE *shrugs.*

CHRISTINE. What were you gonna read? You never told me.

DENISE. Corinthians.

BRADWELL. Bible.

DENISE. Yeah. Letter from St Paul.

BRADWELL. Who to?

DENISE. The Corinthians.

BRADWELL. Oh, right. What did it say?

JIM *appears in the snug/space leading upstairs (unseen by* CHRISTINE *or* DENISE).

CHRISTINE. Go on, it's alright.

A pause.

DENISE. '… although our outer self is wasting away, our inner self is being renewed day by day. For this momentary light affliction is producing for us an eternal weight of glory beyond all comparison, as we look not to what is seen but to what is unseen; for what is seen is transitory, but what is unseen is eternal.'

BRADWELL. Is good, I knew it would be.

DENISE. I know.

BRADWELL *nods.*

CHRISTINE. Terrific.

RUSSELL. Glorious.

After a pause, JIM *returns, towel in hand.*

JIM. No one up there. Deserted. Apart from all the…

JIM *holds out the towel, which* BRADWELL *takes.*

BRADWELL. Oh, thank you, Jim. And, shall I whack a bit of music on? Liven things up a bit? Not too lively though, obviously.

CHRISTINE. Okay then, Bradley.

BRADWELL *nods.*

BRADWELL *approaches the jukebox.*

Where's Nick?

JIM. I thought he was… on Ebay, but.

CHRISTINE. What?

JIM. Nothing. He ain't up there. Maybe hanging from a tree somewhere.

CHRISTINE. Who's serving then?

JIM. I will. If you want.

A brief pause.

CHRISTINE. Okay. Okay. You can be. Barman, or whatever. But… I mean, we'll just get through today, okay?

JIM. Yeah.

CHRISTINE. First. But I don't know about after that, yet.

JIM. Right.

CHRISTINE. I need to think.

JIM. Yeah.

BRADWELL. What a fucking classic!

As BRADWELL *says this, 'True' by Spandau Ballet starts.*

This is a fucking tune, Mr Downing!

RUSSELL. I'm sure.

BRADWELL. Proper legendary.

JIM. I should sort the bar out.

CHRISTINE. Yeah.

CHRISTINE *then goes back to tidying up. After a long-ish pause (with everyone going about their business cleaning, etc.), she finds the cracked iPhone.*

Who's is this?

A brief pause, where JIM, DENISE *and* RUSSELL *all share the moment.*

DENISE. It's… it's Russell's.

CHRISTINE. Is it?

RUSSELL (*standing as he says it*). Yes. Yes yes. It's mine. Definitely mine. Completely.

CHRISTINE. It's all cracked.

RUSSELL. Yeah, I dropped it in a… a bread bin. On a bread bin.

CHRISTINE. Right.

CHRISTINE *hands him the phone.*

RUSSELL. Thank you. Thanks. So much.

JIM. You big oaf.

RUSSELL. Yes. Good song this. Very good fucking song.

RUSSELL *nods.*

BRADWELL. Glad you like it, Mr Downing.

RUSSELL *sits.*

A pause.

RUSSELL. There's something on your sleeve.

DENISE. What?

RUSSELL. Oh no, it's gone. Silly me.

DENISE. Yeah.

RUSSELL *goes back to his crossword.*

BRADWELL (*looking outside*). I think that's all them now.

After a brief pause, JIM *moves towards* RUSSELL *and covertly takes the phone from him, as he says:*

JIM. Russell, prepare yourself, some of those people will make me look like Noël fucking Coward.

RUSSELL. I will Mr Thomas… Jim, thank you.

JIM. Yeah. Brace yourself.

Blackout.

The End.